FIBERGLASS BOAT RESTORATION

THE
PROJECT PLANNING GUIDE

CAPTAIN WAYNE CANNING

SEAHORSE PUBLISHING

Seahorse Publishing books may be purchased in bulk at special discounts for sales promotion, corporate gifts, fund-raising, or educational purposes. Special editions can also be created to specifications. For details, contact the Special Sales Department, Skyhorse Publishing, 307 West 36th Street, 11th Floor, New York, NY 10018 or info@skyhorsepublishing.com.

Seahorse® and Skyhorse Publishing® is a registered trademark of Skyhorse Publishing, Inc.®, a Delaware corporation.

Visit our website at www. skyhorsepublishing.com

10 9 8 7 6 5 4 3 2 1

Library of Congress Cataloging-in-Publication Data is available on file.

Cover design by Tom Lau
Jacket photographs: Wayne Canning

ISBN: 978-1-944824-26-6
Ebook ISBN: 978-1-944824-27-3

Printed in China

Contents

Introduction

O ver the last thirty to forty years, boat builders, both large and small, have produced thousands of fiberglass boats. Fiberglass, unlike many other types of boatbuilding materials, does not rot, rust, or break down over time. In fact, fiberglass continues to cure and become stronger as it ages. As a result, there are now thousands of older, used fiberglass boats available, some in better shape than others. These boats can often be purchased for less than the price of a small used car. Older fiberglass boats can offer a significant bargain over that of a new or recent model used boat. However, it takes selection of the right boat, and careful planning, to truly come out ahead. As world problems, rising energy costs, and political frustration continue to grow, many would-be escapists dream of sailing off to a tropical paradise. Many without large sums of money to spend choose to purchase an older boat as an economical way to their planned adventures. Others simply want to experience the satisfaction of bringing something old back to life, either as a way to show off their skills or to simply enjoy the satisfaction of working with their hands. Additionally, more and more people are looking to live aboard a boat as a way to live near the water in places where most real estate has gotten prohibitively expensive. Project boats offer a way to these dreams; however they are not without their problems and pitfalls. This project planning guide offers information and advice not found in any other do-it-yourself boat repair book. Here you will find the tools and knowledge needed to select the right boat, plan the work, and budget your project for a successful completion.

Whatever the reason for wanting to take on the restoration of a project boat, proper planning and organization can mean the difference between success and failure. This is not a book about how to make a scarf joint or how to rebuild a motor; it is a book about how to put all your skills together in the right order to successfully complete a project boat restoration. It is a guide to getting the work done without getting in over your head and to help avoid the mistakes made by others. It will explain why it is important to put your efforts and resources into some areas and not others. It contains valuable information about what to look for when considering the purchase of a project boat, as well as what to avoid. Although the focus will be on fiberglass boats, this information will be useful to anyone undertaking the building or restoration of any type of project boat. The concepts of planning and organizing the work will apply to many types of boat projects, big or small, so even if you are only planning small improvements or thinking of a complete upgrade you will likely find much of the information within this book helpful.

1 What Is a Project Boat and Is One Right for You?

For those of us with dreams bigger than our bank account, the prospect of owning a boat might seem out of reach. For others, the joys of working on and restoring a boat might be the dream itself. Anyone looking into owning a boat knows only too well the high cost of purchasing a new boat. Sticker shock can be as bracing as that cold winter wave over the bow. But for those who like to work with their hands and have some skills along with the desire to put out the effort, there are alternatives. A project boat might just fit the bill to get you on the water without having to mortgage your life away.

Before getting started, it helps to understand just what a project boat is so you can understand if one is right for you. A project boat can be anything from a small rowboat built from scratch to a mine sweeper converted into a world cruiser. Almost any boat qualifies as a project boat because, let's face it, almost all boats are a project in one way or another. Owners are always adding to or modifying their boats to fit their needs and tastes. In this sense, even a new boat can be considered a project boat of sorts.

For the purpose of this book I will narrow down the definition a bit and primarily focus on older fiberglass boats. That's not to say the information in this book will not be helpful to anyone working on any other type of project boat. Big, small, wood, steel, or fiberglass, the principles are the same, but because the most common project boats are older fiberglass boats, that will be the focus of the information within this book.

The heyday of boat building came in the early sixties and continued through to the mid-nineties. During this period, many boat builders, big and small, opened their doors and began producing hundreds and sometimes thousands of cost-effective fiberglass boats. Because fiberglass molds were relatively easy and inexpensive to construct, builders could produce numerous identical vessels economically using just a few molds and simple tools. The boats produced by these companies ranged in size from small dinghies to large semi-custom yachts. Companies such as Pearson, Catalina, Hatteras and Carver grew to become large corporations by producing quality vessels at affordable prices, thus bringing the boating lifestyle to the middle class. Hundreds of smaller shops also opened their doors, producing limited runs of high-quality (and some not so high-quality) semi-custom boats. All types of vessels were produced, including powerboats, sailboats, trawlers, and commercial vessels. Because many of these early builders did not have the design or engineering expertise of today's builders, they often chose to overbuild. Materials were cheap and the consumer demanded heavy construction, so the tendency was to simply add more material to create a strong vessel.

▲ Early fiberglass boat building.

Thousands of solidly built boats were produced, many still in service today.

Because fiberglass does not rot like wood or rust like steel, many of these boats, even though they may have been neglected or even abandoned, may still be worth saving. Nobody really knows for sure how long a fiberglass boat will last; I have heard lifespans as short as ten or fifteen years to as long as 100 years. The fact is we know there are many boats still in service that are now over fifty-years-old and still going strong. As with many things, how well a boat was constructed and how well it has been cared for has an effect on its overall life span. Suffice it to say, the true lifespan of fiberglass has yet to be fully determined; age alone does not indicate if a boat is worth saving. Combine this with the ever-increasing price of new boats and these older boats may not be such a bad deal after all. Restoring an older boat can often give you a perfectly good vessel

▲ Waiting to be restored.

for a fraction of the cost of a new one. You also get the satisfaction of taking something old and making it new again. The saying "They just don't build them like they used to" really lends itself to older fiberglass boats. In many cases, fully restored older boats may often be even better than new boats because they are heavier built.

The long life of fiberglass, coupled with the surplus of reasonably priced older fiberglass boats on the market, make restoration a tempting prospect. Many decent boats can be had for less than the price of a used car and in some cases even for free. That said, not just any older boat is worth the effort and expense to restore. Later in this book, we will discuss what to look for and what to avoid when selecting a project boat. Picking the right boat will have much to do with the final success of your project. It is also important to understand that any used boat will have a limited resale value no matter how much time and money you put into it. A 1983 Hatteras motor yacht is only going to have a resale value close to what other 1983 Hatteras motor yachts are selling for. It does not matter if you have spent twice that amount on the restoration; it is still only going to be worth so much. This is an important concept you must keep in mind from the start.

Not all project boats are older boats. Many project boat candidates are newer vessels that have been damaged by weather or accidents. These boats are often sold by insurance companies in an effort to recoup their losses. If the estimated cost of repairs comes to more than 80 percent of the insured value of the boat, the insurance companies will often "total" the boat. Some policies mandate the boat be restored to like-new condition, something that may not be possible, which will also result in a total loss being declared. Once the boat is considered a total loss the insurance company will pay the owner for the full insured value and take ownership. The insurance company will then sell the damaged boat in an effort to recoup some of their losses. Sometimes the owner will buy the boat back from the insurance company and use some of the settlement funds to make repairs. Most often, though,

▲ There is some truth here.

the boat is sold for salvage value. These damaged boats often make good candidates for repair but care needs to be taken. We will talk more about this in Chapter 3.

A project boat is a dream waiting to happen and, like most dreams, every project boat is as unique as its owner. All it takes is vision, hard work, and a bit of money to get there. Unfortunately, many more have the dream than have the time and resources to see it through to the end. Most project boats will take a lot more time and money to complete than their owners ever expected. Purchasing a project boat thinking you will end up with a high-end yacht for a fraction of the cost is a mistake many have made. Nothing in life comes without a price and this is especially true of most project boats. The odds of success will often depend on how realistic the owner is. I have seen many more failures with project boats than successes. The biggest reason for failure by far is unrealistic expectations of the time and money required to complete the project. I say this not to discourage anyone, but rather to point out that this journey will not be as easy as some might expect. That is not to say it will not be worth the effort but, like most things, understanding what you are getting into before you start will help you succeed. That, after all, is the goal of this book; to help you succeed where others have failed and to help guide you through and around many of the pitfalls others have fallen into.

Before starting on any project boat, the first thing that must be determined is whether or not a project boat is right for you, or better yet whether YOU are right for a project boat. Not everyone is suited to the task of restoring an older or damaged boat. It takes many hours of free time and more money than expected to bring a boat back to good condition. It can be a challenge, but that, after all, is part of the reason for taking on a project boat; the satisfaction of using your skills and abilities to finish something you can be proud of. It can be very rewarding and satisfying to bring an old boat back from the scrap heap and turn her into something to take pride in. In addition, it is possible to save money over the cost of buying a finished boat, but it takes careful planning and a lot of hard work to really come out ahead.

The single biggest reason most people take on a project boat is to save money. This alone is a poor reason to undertake such a task. Yes, you can save money, but you can likewise lose money and the sad truth is many more lose than save. If you want to save money, you will undoubtedly have to put in many hours of your own time and labor. However long you think it may take to do something on a boat, it always seems to take three to four times as long as expected. After more than forty years building and repairing boats, I am always amazed at how long it can take to do even the simplest of tasks. It is also possible to save money with careful sourcing of parts and materials. Keep in mind that sourcing parts also takes time, effort, and careful planning. It is very easy to get carried away and spend more than you expected when it comes to parts and supplies. Many

▲ A restoration in progress.

seemingly good deals may not be so good in the long run. Careful planning and discipline will help you reduce the cost. If your sole reason for restoring a boat is to save money you will likely be disappointed.

Others take on a project boat simply because they love the work. This is one of the better reasons for working on a project boat. Let's face it, most boat restorations will demand the best of your time and skills. If you love the work it will keep you motivated for the long run. Restoring a boat as a hobby can be very rewarding. It can challenge your skills as well as force you to learn new ones. If you enjoy getting your hands dirty and constantly being challenged, then a boat restoration might be just the thing for you. Large or small, completing a project boat can be a very satisfying experience. Doing the work yourself also gives you finite control over the quality and direction of the project. You can have complete control over the level of fit and finish to your satisfaction. There is also the fact that you will be intimately familiar with your boat, which can be very useful when it comes to making repairs in the future. For many, restoring boats it is not even about ever using the boat; it is more about having something to do, a project to work on. I have known some who never take their boats off the dock, yet work on them all the time. Spending an afternoon varnishing fine woodwork can be very Zen-like, offering a relaxing afternoon away from the rush and worry of everyday life. Sitting back at the end of the day with a cold beer admiring your labor can be very satisfying indeed.

Then there are the project boats that you just sort of end up with when you were not really looking. I think of this more as the boat finding you than you finding the boat, sort of like a lost puppy or kitten. It could be a boat that a buddy gave you or maybe you put in a low bid at an auction thinking you would never win and then end up winning. Perhaps you are just strolling the docks and suddenly see the boat of your dreams, love at first sight, not unlike that cute blonde you once fell in love with as a teenager! As with that pretty blonde, your heart has taken over your brain and before you know it your checkbook is out and there is no turning back. It is then that reality kicks in and you find yourself with more than you bargained for. Of course, by then it is simply too late and you have to see her through to the end. Some folks I have known ended up with their project when a family member or friend passed away. These folks felt they needed to finish the project to honor that loved one. One person I knew, after inheriting a half-finished boat from a friend, not only finished the boat, but then spent several years cruising in it to completely fulfill his lost friend's dreams. Surprisingly, these unplanned projects often are the most successful. Whether honoring a loved one or due to a weakness of the heart, these owners seem to stay motivated.

For some, a project boat offers a way of controlling costs. It can make sense to purchase a cheaper boat and then put money into her when you can rather than taking out a large loan and its associated payments for a finished boat. With a project boat you can spend money when you have it and not spend it when you don't. This is often a good option when looking at a fixer upper that is usable but is still in need of upgrades and repairs. This can also be a good choice when thinking of doing long-range cruising in the future. You can still use the boat and get to know all the systems while deciding where best to spend your money and time. With today's uncertain economy this can also offer some security, knowing that if your financial situation changes you can put a brake on the boat-spending until things improve.

Whatever the reason for taking on a project boat, for it to be successful it is important to understand your abilities and limitations. Planning is the key to the success for any project and the first step in any planning is to understand just what you are getting into and how you will go about it. If you have more time than money, you will need to have the skills required to complete most of the work yourself. If you have more money than time, you may want to plan on hiring help to get things done. It is important to look at all these things realistically. If you have never worked

▲ Enjoying the work.

with your hands and have few hands-on skills it would be foolish to just assume you can do all the work required. Likewise, if you are short on funds, do not underestimate the costs of parts and supplies involved. There are ways around these obstacles but being realistic up front will help.

If you are good with your hands and enjoy the work then you will be able to save a lot of money by doing most of the work yourself. If you are not good with your hands or have never done much "hands on" type work it is important to be realistic about how much you really can do without paying for help. A rare few come by these skills naturally, for most it can take years to fully become proficient at a particular skill. Boat restoration requires many skills, including fiberglass, carpentry, electrical, plumbing, painting, and mechanical skills, just to name a few. There are many hats to be worn when working on a project boat. If you have some skills but are lacking in others such as mechanical or electrical, these can often be learned at local community colleges. Some coastal schools may even have a boat-building or repair program. These classes can often be taken in the evening, making it a practical way to obtain needed knowledge. If you have little hands-on experience it might be best to start small and test yourself. Get a small dinghy or outboard-type boat and see how it goes. See what your skill sets are before getting too deeply involved in a larger project. This is also a great way to learn if you will enjoy this type of work if you have never done it before. Better to make mistakes on a small-scale project than to put all your resources into a large project you may not want to finish. Starting small will test almost all of the skills needed in a bigger project without getting in over your head. If you have worked on boats before, either your own or a friend's, you might be able to jump right into a bigger project, but if you are completely new to boat work, I strongly recommend you start small.

It is important to remember this kind of work is not for everyone and it takes a special type of person to really enjoy all the challenges you will face. These include spending endless hours of grinding fiberglass

▲ Working hard.

while sweating in Tyvek suits and breathing through a full face mask, all while working in unnatural positions with lousy light in all kinds of weather, and spending all your free time laboring away at dirty and often boring tasks. You will make mistakes and be overwhelmed and exhausted both physically and mentally. Everything will take longer and cost more than you expected, but you will be rewarded in the end by knowing you had what it takes to do what few can.

As with most things in life, money is important to success and this is true with a project boat as well. Having the required skills will save you money in labor, but you still need to purchase parts and supplies. At times you may need to hire outside labor as well for things you may not have the skills or tools for, such as welding. There can be additional costs as well, for example storage, insurance, launching fees, and the list goes on. Before starting, you need to have some understanding of the cash flow needed to keep your project moving forward. Many grossly underestimate the expense and end up stalling or worse never finishing at all, solely due to the lack of sufficient funding. Thinking about money and planning a budget should be one of your first considerations before starting a boat restoration. This is one area where

▲ A big project.

it is important to remain realistic and, if anything, try to overestimate, rather than underestimate. You should plan for unexpected expenses, because you will surely have them. I will talk more about finances and budgeting in Chapter 6, but it is an important consideration before you start. It will also be an important factor in selecting a suitable boat. Although a sixty-footer may seem tempting, if you cannot afford the slip rent, it makes little sense to attempt something that big. I know this seems obvious but time and again I have seen people make just such a mistake. It is all too easy to convince yourself that you will figure it out as you go along, but do not kid yourself. Setting up a monthly budget will help keep you on track and give you an idea of what you can and cannot afford before you start. Knowing this will help you avoid getting in over your head from the beginning.

"Time waits for no man" and this is particularly true when it comes to a project boat. Understanding your available free time is an important consideration before starting a project boat. As with money, time can be a very limited resource. The bigger the project, the more free time it will suck up, so understanding just how much time you can and are willing to dedicate is important. If you are wealthy and hiring others to do the work, this may not be an issue, but few taking on a project boat have the money to pay for all of the labor. It may seem like you have plenty of free time on your hands, but I can assure you there is never enough when it comes to working on a boat. Family, job, and other hobbies will all place demands on your free time as well. If you are retired or only have to work part-time this may not be as much of a problem, but for those working full-time with families and friends, your free time becomes precious indeed. It is important to be realistic about just how much free time you will have to put into your project. Again this is a good reason to try a small project before tackling that fifty-footer you have always dreamed of. Any project boat larger than twenty feet can easily take years to complete. The bigger the boat, the more time it will take. As mentioned before, everything takes longer than expected when working on boats, so planning for this from the start will save you a lot of frustration and disappointment. You must plan for the unexpected and leave windows of time open if you're planning to avoid frustration and disappointment. If you are lucky and do not hit too many unexpected problems, or as a former employer of mine used to call them "opportunities," you will finish ahead of schedule rather than behind. On the other hand, if you do not plan for them, you are likely to get behind and get discouraged. Like they say, "time is money," and this can be true with a boat restoration. The longer it takes, the more you will spend on dockage, storage, insurance, and other items.

Motivation and, more importantly, staying motivated is important as well. It is easy to get psyched up when you first start a project, but keeping that enthusiasm over the long term is a bit harder. Some people come by this naturally, but for others it takes a bit of work. Most project boats can take a long time to complete, often years.

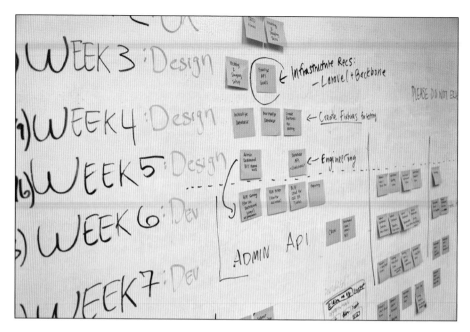

▲ Planning for time. *Photo courtesy of Pexels.com*

It can be difficult to maintain a good positive attitude for a long time. Setbacks and disappointments are to be expected in any large project. It is important to avoid getting frustrated or discouraged when you encounter them. Be realistic; think about your personality and whether you feel you can hang in for the long haul. Are you the type of person that will stay self-motivated? Your motivation for starting your project will have an effect on how well you maintain your enthusiasm over the length of the project. This is one reason those that inherit a project boat do so well. They have a strong motivation and desire to complete the project. Whether your desire is to sail around the world or simply to go fishing, you need to make sure your motivation is strong enough to see you through to the end.

Depending on the length and scope of your project, you also need to consider your professional and personal situation. Scanning the boats listed on eBay, I often see half-finished boats for sale with the seller stating they are selling due to job transfer, divorce, or some other personal situation that prevents them from completing the project. It can often be hard to predict such changes in your personal life, but knowing you are in a stable situation before starting a big project is helpful. There are ways to help minimize the problems caused by a sudden life change. The most important of these is getting the boat in a condition where it can be moved if need be. I will talk more about this in Chapter 5 but it is good to keep in mind from the start that it may, at some point, become necessary to move your project to a new location. Of course a failing marriage or poor health is usually impossible to predict but it helps to keep in mind that these things can and do happen. No one wants to think the worst, but it is something to keep in mind if you are embarking on a large project that could take years to complete.

I have also heard of more than one project boat that has caused a serious rift in a marriage. If married, make sure your spouse is onboard for the project, even better if they are willing to help or partner with you. A project boat can consume a large amount of free time, so before starting, make sure this commitment will not adversely affect others in your life. Of course, the best situation is when others in your life are participating in your project. A project boat can be a great way to bring people together, working as a team for the end goal. It likewise can tear people apart if they cannot work together or are not working for the same goal. As suggested earlier, I would recommend trying a small project first if you have never done anything like this as a team. The rewards of working together with family or friends can be very gratifying indeed.

Taking care of your own health is equally important. This is important both physically and mentally. Heath issues can quickly put an end to a well-planned project. One of the saddest cases I know of was where a young man building a cold-molded trimaran took his own life halfway through the project. It was thought that the constant exposure to the chemicals involved had an adverse effect on his mental health. Whether or not this is true, it points out the need to take care of both your physical and mental health as you proceed.

▲ A complete project.

Stress and injuries can also slow things down or bring them to a stop. Working on project boats can expose you to many hazards; do not neglect using proper safety practices while working.

As you can see, there is a lot to think about before taking on a project boat. My goal is to help you avoid the common pitfalls and "opportunities" that can and do derail many projects. Success depends on many factors. Staying motivated and enthusiastic is the result of being prepared and aware of possible problems before they are encountered. It is important to work within your abilities and resources to avoid getting in over your head. Knowing what you are getting into is the best way to avoid disappointment. Completing a project boat can be very satisfying; you will get to know your boat inside and out while at the same time taking pride in the fruits of your efforts. If you work as a team with others you can share this rewarding experience with them as well. A project boat can be fun but it can also be frustrating and challenging. No two project boats are alike and no two owners are alike. This is what makes restoring a project boat such an interesting and rewarding experience. Tackling a project boat can be a bit like climbing a mountain—it is an uphill battle but the view from the top can be very rewarding!

2 Logistics

L ike the UPS commercials have said, it's all about logistics. This not only applies to moving packages around the globe, it applies equally as well to a project boat. Logistics are more than just moving stuff around, though; it includes everything from where to keep a project boat to how to launch her when complete and all the little bits and pieces in between. Logistics can often make or break a project before it is even started.

There is much to consider before starting work on a project boat. Where will you keep her while doing the work? What tools and supplies will be needed and where will you keep those tools and

▲ Boat parts on their way.

supplies? Will you have to work inside or outside and what effect will weather play? What special equipment will be needed and will that equipment be available locally? Then there are the legal issues such as insurance, zoning regulations, and liability to consider as well. All this needs to be taken into account if your project is to be successful.

One of the very first logistical challenges is where to keep your project boat while working on it. Should your project boat be on land or in the water? What is locally available for either of these choices? What are the advantages and disadvantages of each choice? Selecting the right location can often make or break a project, so careful consideration is needed. Smaller boats tend to be easy but the larger the project, the harder it will be to find the best work location.

When considering alternatives for a project work location it should be kept in mind that the closer you live to the work site, the more work will get done. It is by far easier to get a couple extra hours of boat work in after a day on the "real job" if the boat is close at hand. It is also one of those unavoidable, unwritten rules that the further

▲ A typical boatyard.

away from the boat you live, the less work will get done. Any distance more than an hour's drive or so is likely going to be too far. Many try to convince themselves otherwise but the reality is the further away you are from the boat, the longer it will take to complete. It helps to be realistic when considering this. Additionally, travel time to and from the boat is time better spent working on the boat. The closer it is to home base, the better.

There are several distinct advantages to working on a project boat on land rather than in the water. The most obvious is that you will be able to work on the bottom, underwater fittings, and the hull topsides while on land. There are also other reasons it is better to be on land. Being able to park your vehicle near or next to the boat can be a real advantage. Less time will be spent going back and forth to retrieve tools and parts. Storing parts, particularly large parts, under the boat can save time and money as well. If you are able to work on

▲ A project in storage yard.

your boat in a shed or alongside a workshop you will have all your shop tools and bulk supplies close at hand. Even if you cannot have the boat close to a shop it is often possible to have a small portable storage unit or enclosed trailer nearby for tools and supplies. Another advantage to land storage is you do not have to worry about the boat sinking. However, you must make sure to keep rainwater out or the boat can "sink" on land.

If you own your own house or have property, keeping the boat there could make sense. By doing that, you will not have to pay rent or storage. There are some things you need to consider before planning on bringing your project home. In many neighborhoods a project boat may not be a welcome sight. Many communities have rules against boats (even small ones) and RVs in yards or driveways. So unless you have property a bit off the beaten path or are sure that there are no restrictions, this may not be an option. If you live in a housing development it is best to check with the homeowners association first. Those with small farms or rural property will likely not have this problem but you should still check local ordinances before getting in too deep. If you rent a home or an apartment, keeping the boat where you live will likely not be an option, but it never hurts to ask, particularly if you rent in a rural location.

If you do not own your own property or restrictions prevent you from keeping a project boat at that location, there are other options that may work. If you live close to a boatyard or marina this could be a good choice. Not all boatyards allow do-it-yourself work so ask first. Those that do may charge an extra fee for the owner or outside helpers to work on the boat while on their property. Some charge a daily fee per person that can add up fast. Most will also require you carry, at minimum, liability insurance. It is important to find out all of a boatyard's rules before signing on the dotted line. Let the yard management know in advance you have a project boat and find out if they have any additional fees associated with that. Do not wait until the project is in full swing to find out they have been charging you forty dollars a day per person for outside help. I have talked

▲ In the works.

with many owners who have gotten into trouble with the boatyard because they did not fully understand the rules. If you think you will be doing any sandblasting or spray painting make sure you know about restrictions or requirements before starting this type of work. Most yards require tenting if you do so, while others simply do not allow it. Many smaller yards may not have written rules so it is always best to ask upfront and have a clear understanding of what you can and cannot do.

Make sure you can get along with the boatyard management before committing as well. It can be costly to have to move a project midway through the work simply because the manager is not cooperative. Most boatyards are private property, the owners and managers set the rules and the boat owners have to follow them or leave. Not all managers are reasonable and some make the rules up as they go. It is always a good idea to talk to other boat owners in the yard to find out how easy it is to deal with the management and just how DIY-friendly they really are. Going out of your way to be friendly to management can pay off in the long run. Occasionally getting doughnuts and coffee for the yard crew and office staff can gain you brownie points that can pay off later.

Another plus to working in a boatyard is that many will have a small store for basic supplies such as paints, solvents, and fasteners. Although the prices might be higher, it can be a time-saver when you just need a couple of ¼-inch bolts to finish a task. Many yards will allow you to park small storage trailers or even place a shipping container near the boat, making it convenient to have parts and tools close at hand. Most will charge an additional fee for this but it may well be worth it. Many smaller boatyards are friendly enough that they will offer advice or even let you borrow some tools, providing you return them promptly. Perks like that can be a real lifesaver and worth the extra money a boatyard may cost over other storage options. Additionally, there may be other owners working on project boats nearby. These folks may lend a hand when you have a job that requires two or more people. In return, you can help them when needed. Most boatyards will have basic facilities including bathrooms and showers. Never underestimate the value of a good shower after having spent all day in a Tyvek suit grinding fiberglass.

Boatyards are not the only locations available to work on a project boat. Most communities now have an abundance of storage yards offering many options. Not all facilities will allow you to work on your boat while there, so this should be your first question when checking into one of these locations. These storage yards can be just simple fenced-in lots or more complete facilities offering covered or indoor storage. The drawback to these places is that many do not have electricity or running water available. They do usually offer good security and may be a good option if it's closer to where you live. Many storage facilities will also have small garage storage units that can come in handy for keeping tools and supplies on-site. If power is not available, a small portable generator could be used.

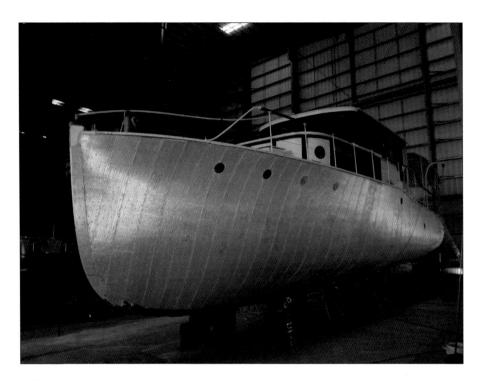

▲ Working in an old warehouse.

In some towns you may be able to find an old warehouse that has been converted to storage and workspaces. These warehouses often have high ceilings and are generally rented by the square foot, making this is an interesting option for an indoor workspace. Most warehouses are not heated and may have restrictions on spray painting and sandblasting but are worth checking into as you would never have to worry about rain and wind. Some may even have overhead hoists available which could come in handy. These warehouses generally have good security as well, making them an interesting option to consider.

You could also keep your project at a friend or relative's property. I am sure you are aware of some of the problems you might encounter if you choose this option. If considering this route, make sure you have a good long-term relationship with the person who owns the property. There should be a clear understanding about expectations and any restrictions they may have. If close to a home or house, use common sense and do not operate loud tools or noisy equipment during early or late hours of the day. Be sure to respect the privacy of your host and check with them before starting any major work such as sandblasting or bringing in heavy equipment.

Keeping the boat in water can make sense if it is close to where you live or you think the boat will need to be moved before the work is complete. I have found it is often harder to work on a boat while it is in the water for several reasons. The first problem is you cannot work on anything below the waterline. This can sometimes slow work down, particularly when it comes to working on underwater fittings. The second problem is many marinas will not allow work on a boat while in the slip. Some older marinas or boatyards may be a bit more tolerant but many do not allow it anymore. Neighbors may complain about sanding or painting near their boats as well. The docks will need to be kept clear and you will have to be careful about spilling paint or damaging the docks. You will spend more time walking back and forth to your vehicle for tools and parts because storage is often further away. Some marinas will supply or allow you to have a dock box which will help some for storing tools and parts. If you do stay in the water, try to get a slip as close to the dock ramp and parking lot as possible. If you can find a bulkhead where you can drive up close to the boat it will really save time. It is amazing how much time and energy can be wasted walking up and down a dock. Some marinas will allow you to keep a small cargo trailer or other storage unit on the property but it is best to check with management ahead of time. A few marinas will even have some storage units available with the slip or for rent. These can be very useful for keeping tools and supplies in. Keep in mind security issues when storing parts and tools as well.

Being in the water does make it easier to test gear and equipment, such as running engines and pumps. If the scope of the work is not too involved it may be possible to use the boat while working on it as well. I have found it can be a big morale booster to be able to take the boat out every now and then while working on it. Spending

▲ Project in the water.

a day relaxing on the boat rather than working on it will boost your motivation. If you are not planning on using the boat while in the water it is still important to maintain enough of the boat's electrical system to keep the bilge pumps and other critical equipment running and batteries charged.

Whether you keep the boat on land or in the water, make sure you will be able to get the boat to the location where you plan to work on it. For boats in the water this means checking depths in the marina as well as its entrance channel. Think about how you will get there; will it come under its own power or need to be towed? Unless you have a tow boat available, towing services can be expensive. Towing requires the boat to be at least somewhat seaworthy and a good weather window will have to be considered. Moving a project boat over anything but a short distance by water can prove challenging, but is not impossible. I have patched large holes with plywood and moved the boat more than a hundred miles but it does require careful planning.

If the boat is to be kept on land and you are moving it by truck there are several things to think about. For small projects that will be on a boat trailer, things tend to be pretty simple. If you do not have a truck to tow the boat or it is simply too far away, a transporter can be hired. Small boats on trailers can often be moved by a company that specializes in transporting cars. If only a local move is needed, a tow truck company can often help. Just make sure the trailer is up to the task first. Check the tires and wheel bearings as well as the brakes. Make sure the trailer is strong enough for the trip; it can be expensive to have to recover a boat and broken trailer from the highway. Highway patrol usually doesn't have a sense of humor when traffic is being blocked by a broken down old boat and trailer.

For larger boats and long distance moves, a shipper who specializes in yacht transport may be needed. There are many companies large and small to help with this. Most are reputable but not all, so it is important to get references and check them. Make sure you understand all the fees involved so there will be no surprises at the end of the move. Does the shipper's insurance cover you or will you need your own? Try to keep the timing of things like travel lifts or cranes for loading and unloading flexible. Trucks deal with the same traffic we do and may not be able to show up at an exact time or even exact day. It is up to the boat owner to arrange loading and unloading so think about this at the beginning. Some transporters will be able to do this with a hydraulic trailer and this is an option worth checking into. If the boat is not in a boatyard with a lift or will be going to a boatyard without a lift, you may need to hire a crane to load or unload it. The shipper can provide advice but, in the end, this will be up to you. Make sure the transport company will handle all the road permits and routing needed. For larger boats this can get tricky and it is worth hiring a company that has done this type of work before to handle the details. Do not assume anything

▲ Backing into tight location. *Photo by Nikko Lorenczi.*

and ask lots of questions before hiring a transporter. Before even talking to you, most transporters will require the basic dimensions of the boat. Measure from the keel to the highest part of the boat that is not removable, the overall length of the boat, and the widest part of the boat. Do not use published information on the boat—go out and measure it yourself. With some boats, things such as flying bridges may need to be removed so plan for this in advance. A good experienced shipper will be able to offer a lot of good advice.

Make sure the truck and trailer will be able to get to where you want to locate the boat. The bigger the boat, the more complicated this all becomes. The drivers will know the highways but local roads and driveways at each end can pose a challenge. Check for low power lines, bridges, and other overhead obstacles. Trees can sometimes be trimmed but low bridges and power lines are not so easy to move. Sharp turns and humps in the road or driveway can become problems as well. Large trailers tend to be low to the ground and will not go over even small short hills or humps. Sharp turns can be impossible to navigate for a large truck as well. If you are using a professional transporter and are in doubt, ask them to look at the chosen route. I have seen more than one plan fall apart when the boat would not fit down a driveway, or worse, get stuck halfway down. Don't assume that access to a boatyard will be easy either. I have seen trucks get stuck there as well.

Once a good work location has been selected and you have figured out how to get your project boat there, it is time to think about insurance. Although you may not think you would need insurance on a project boat you will at least want some form of liability insurance. Many marinas and boatyards now require this and it makes sense for your own protection. If working on the boat at your home this may not be a problem as you may be covered under your homeowner's policy. Check with your agent before assuming you are covered. If you are going to be renting a location, you will likely be required to carry some form of liability insurance. Like it or not, we live in a world where being sued is a real possibility so having liability insurance is a must. If someone gets injured on or around your boat you can be held liable even if it is not your fault.

Insurance for a project boat can be hard to get so it helps to start thinking about this early and find out what options are available before you need it. Few insurance companies are interested in insuring a project boat. The problem is, most insurance companies see project boats as high risk for low return. This is because they base their premiums on the overall value of the boat and most project boats have a low value to start with. If the value of the boat is low, it might be easier to just get liability insurance but even this can be hard to get. It will take some shopping around but it can be done. If your project boat is more than ten years old and bigger than around twenty feet, you will likely need a survey before the insurance company will even talk to you. This is to establish value and condition. Of course a survey will show the boat is not complete and may have many deficiencies. To get around this, you can request port insurance or builders insurance which will insure you while the vessel is being worked on in port. With port insurance, the boat is still covered but has restrictions on going anywhere. This means you are only insured in port until you get a clean survey. Exceptions can be made to move the boat to another marina or within the same marina for haul out and such. This can be a good option if you need insurance beyond liability. Insurance may also be easier to get with a boat stored on land as the insurance companies see this as a safer risk due to the fact the boat cannot sink. Some insurance companies will issue builder's insurance as well. This will cover both the value of the boat as well as liability. As work proceeds and money is spent, the boat will become worth more so be sure to update your policy to reflect this. This may require an updated survey. Having a good agent will help in finding the best policy for your needs.

With a location picked out and insurance in place it will be time to think about where to store all the boat parts not needed right away as well as tools and supplies. Much of this will depend on the scope and extent of the project and how big the project boat is. The bigger the

▲ Parts stored in a container.

boat and the more work being done the more storage will be needed. Even smaller project boats can require a surprisingly large amount of storage space for parts, supplies, and equipment. Having storage for all this close at hand will be helpful. Nothing is more frustrating than getting started on a job and finding you left an important part or tool at another location. The more that can be kept close at hand the less time will be wasted retrieving things.

You will also need a storage place for materials that will not be needed until the project is near completion. This would include interior cushions, fenders, lines, sails, electronics, and so on. All this will not be needed for months or possibly years so it needs to be stored in a safe place. As most packages say "store in a cool dry place"; this applies equally to boat parts as well. Bugs and rodents have been known to wreak havoc on stored cushions and sails as well as electronics. The last thing anybody wants to find when nearing completion of a project is that sails or cushions have become a nest for a family of rats and are now useless. Thinking about this ahead of time can save a lot of grief later.

Attics can work well for safe long-term storage but be careful about heat as attics can get very hot in summer months. Heat can be particularly harmful to plastics and electronics. Attached garages can be a good option for long-term storage, particularly if heated and dry. Detached buildings are often not a good choice unless well-sealed and climate-controlled. Your typical garden tool shed is a poor choice for storage as these provide little protection from temperature extremes and critters. Store soft goods in labeled plastic boxes for protection. Taping the lids all the way around will add an additional level of protection, but keep in mind rodents can and will chew through plastic boxes. Larger items such as cushions can be wrapped in plastic for some protection. Avoid storing anything in cardboard boxes as these attract bugs and will often break open with age. If storing any liquids or paints make sure they will not freeze in the winter. The further north you live the more important this becomes. Be careful when storing flammables; these should be stored where they will be away from occupied buildings. For a large project, long-term stored parts can add up to thousands of dollars' worth of equipment so it is important to make sure they will be safe. Think about insurance for stored gear and equipment as well; once again, your homeowners insurance may cover this if stored at home. If storing equipment in a paid storage unit, check if the building owner's insurance covers you. Most will not and many now require you carry your own renter's insurance. It can help to have an inventory and photos of what you have in storage, should you need to file a claim. This can also help you remember what you have and where it is located. Along with photos, a list of what you have and where it is located can be very helpful as well.

Short-term storage of tools and supplies requires greater accessibility for daily use. For an average-sized project an enclosed cargo trailer can make sense. These can be found in many sizes to suit your needs; additionally, the ease with which they can be moved can be helpful as well. I have found by keeping my tools and basic supplies in a small cargo trailer I do not have to worry about forgetting that critical item at home or back at the shop. Basic supplies such as glues, solvents, and fasteners are always nearby when kept on-site. These trailers are also useful should a large part such as an engine need transporting. Because they are covered and lockable they keep everything safe and dry as well. Once again it is important to keep freezing temperatures in mind when storing supplies in trailers. Most boatyards will allow you to keep a small trailer on-site but it is best to ask first. Some will charge an additional fee for this but it may well be worth it. Taking the trailer home with you is a good option allowing you to place needed supplies and equipment in it for the next task at hand when returning to the boat.

▲ A container for storage.

For larger projects, renting or purchasing a used shipping container can be a good option for storage. Used shipping containers are dry and sealed well, keeping rodents and most bugs out. Some containers are large enough that the back end of the container can be used for storage while the front is used as a small workshop with a work bench. The drawback is they are harder to move and most yards will charge extra to have one on-site, if they allow it at all. The convenience may well make it worth paying a bit more, though. Containers are particularly good if you own your property as you will not have to pay extra rent. Shipping containers are available in several sizes and most suppliers will deliver to your site as part of the purchase or rental agreement. Standard sizes are twenty or forty feet long but other sizes can be found. Although not cheap, these do make for a great instant building and are less expensive than traditional buildings. For really large projects they can even be stacked. Containers and cargo trailers can also be resold when the project is complete.

Once you get your project to the work location and storage worked out, the next thing to think about is safe access to the boat while you are working on it. If the boat is on land you will want to be able to get on and off safely and easily. Ladders tend to be dangerous; it is hard to carry tools and supplies up and down a ladder while holding on at the same time. If the project will take more than a couple of weeks, steps or stairs may be worth considering. A set of steps placed alongside the boat will make getting on and off much easier and safer. Using steps or stairs will also keep both hands free for carrying tools and supplies on and off the boat. Steps are also less fatiguing than climbing a ladder. After what can seem like a thousand trips up and down a ladder, steps start to look pretty good. Steps can be purchased from most industrial supply sources or you can build your own. Most lumber yards sell precut risers, making building a set of stairs fairly easy. For short-term use, work stairs can be rented from an industrial tool rental company. If a ladder is to be used, make sure it is in good condition, securely set on solid ground, and tied to the boat at the top. When working on the hull topsides, scaffolding can be easier and safer to work from. Scaffolding can be store-bought, homemade, or even rented when only needed short-term. Avoid the use of oil drums and other less stable work supports. It is important to use common sense when working above ground as falls are the single biggest safety issue and largest cause of injuries and deaths when working on a boat.

If possible, it helps to have a shop to work out of for all the little bits and pieces of the boat that can be removed. Even if the shop is small and only consists of a work bench and vise, it will be helpful. I used to have a small shop in my garage and would take doors, drawers, and trim back to the garage for re-varnishing in the evenings after work at the real job. Doing just a little every evening made a big difference in getting the project done. Quite a bit of work can be done off the boat so the more space available to work the better. This becomes even more important if the boat is a bit further from your home. For larger projects, having some shop tools such as a table saw and drill press can be invaluable as well. A shop can also provide a good place to store raw materials such as lumber and plywood.

It helps to develop good sources for parts and supplies early on. Most coastal towns will have marine wholesalers that service the local boatyards. Although they generally only sell to businesses, it never hurts to talk to them and let them know you are working on a project boat. They may set up an account to give you a source of discount parts and supplies. These wholesalers can be a great source for expendable supplies and paints as well as standard marine parts. One catch to this is that they may require you have a state sales tax account. This can be more trouble than it is worth but never hurts to check into it. It may also pay to talk to your local marine supply and hardware stores as well. Let them know you have a project boat you are working on and see if they can give you a discount for getting most of your supplies through them. Online parts suppliers can be another good source for discount supplies but do require a bit more preplanning to allow for shipping times. Even with shipping costs most online sources will save you money over the traditional local brick and mortar stores.

Used parts can be another great way to save money when sourcing what's needed. Many coastal towns will have a marine consignment shop or two which can not only be a good source of parts but they are just plain fun to browse around in. There are a few larger regional used part stores but I never had much luck with getting them to ship anything and often their prices are not as good as one would hope. That said, these stores may offer an alternative to other traditional sources. Craigslist can be a good source as well but you do need to use a bit more care when shopping on there. That said, I have gotten a few good deals from sellers on Craigslist. EBay is a very good source of parts and supplies both new and used. Using their payment system is very safe for a buyer. EBay is the mother of all online yard sales and this is true for boat parts as well. You can find almost any part needed, big or small. It is not perfect and I sometimes see people getting caught up in the bidding and end up paying more than an item was worth or could have been purchased for elsewhere. Some sellers have high shipping costs so be sure to check those before bidding. It takes time and patience to get good deals on eBay. Plan ahead and take the time to watch regularly and sooner or later you will find the parts needed at a reasonable price. I have purchased everything from electronics and hardware to complete masts with rigging but it can take time to find just that right part. There are numerous new part sellers on eBay as well. Many of these are new businesses just trying to get started while others may be established companies liquidating old stock. Both can offer good deals.

Although some are able to do it, living aboard while restoring a boat is not something I personally recommend. Tools, dust, and dirt get everywhere and the smells of fiberglass and other chemicals can make living aboard very challenging. It is by no means impossible but will add to the difficulty. If you have to live aboard while restoring, it is best to work just one small area at a time. The bigger the boat, the easier this becomes. If living aboard, you will want to have the boat

▲ Disposing of waste.

in the water as this makes life easier and most yards will not allow anyone to stay aboard while the boat is on land.

Finally, do not forget about how you will handle waste. This is not always as easy as it may at first appear. Project boats tend to generate a fair amount of waste and some of it can be toxic. Most local trash services will not deal with things like used solvents and paints. Some boatyards will have disposal for this type of waste. Used motor oil and batteries can be brought to many local auto parts stores for disposal. Solid waste can usually be disposed of at a local landfill for a small tipping fee. Many metals such as aluminum, copper, and lead can be recycled, often giving you a nice bit of extra cash in the process, so save scrap metals for recycling. Teak is becoming an ever harder commodity to come by so it is good to recycle as much of it as possible as well. Last time I checked teak was selling for more than forty dollars per board foot so it pays not to waste any. Take care to think about the environment when disposing of anything harmful and try to recycle when possible.

Keep in mind that all these logistics are important to the success of any project. As they say, the devil is in the details. It is all too easy to focus on the big and often more fun aspects of a project but the little pieces are what pull it all together.

3 Purchasing a Project Boat

One of the first questions most would-be project boat restorers ask is "Where can I find a good deal on a project boat?" There really is no simple answer to this and as with purchasing any boat, it all depends. Project boats can be found pretty much anyplace you find boats, although some places are better than others. There are also some specialized places, such as online auction houses, that handle liquidating damaged boats for insurance companies. Finding the right project boat can be a bit challenging but it is not all that much different than finding any other used boat. It takes a bit of looking around by exploring marinas and other places

▲ Is it a good deal?

you find boats. Of course, that can be part of the fun, exploring marinas and boatyards, poking about in older boats or damaged boats. A project boat is a bit of an adventure and finding the right boat is just part of that experience.

Of course it helps to know just what type of boat you are looking for and how you plan to use it before you start. Many dream of sailing off to far away exotic locations while others may be more interested in finding a small classic outboard to tow behind their classic muscle car. Knowing what you want before starting your search will help narrow things down a bit. This is where you should do a bit of research to narrow down brands and models that might fit your needs. This may not be an issue for those who are better versed in boats, but for beginners it helps to know just what best suits your needs. After all, nobody wants to put in a lot of time, effort, and money only to find in the end the boat they just restored is not really the boat they wanted. Take the time to think about this before starting the search.

Despite what you may have heard, size is important. One of the biggest mistakes made when selecting a project boat to restore is going too large. While it may seem like a great idea to have a sixty-foot ketch to sail off into the sunset, keep in mind that the amount of work and cost increases exponentially as the boat size increases. I have seen many more larger project boat failures than smaller ones. It is all too easy to get in over your head only to find you do not have the time or resources to complete a larger restoration. This is another reason I suggest starting with a small project to test your skills before moving on to a more larger boat. That's not to say a larger restoration cannot be done, but if you are considering anything over forty feet you should be sure you fully understand what you are getting into.

Before getting too excited and running out to find your dream boat, it helps to understand that not all boats in need of repair make good project boats. Making a bad choice can cost you money and, in some cases, make success all but impossible. When selecting a potential project there are some important things to keep in mind. Foremost is what the boat will be worth when it is finished and what will it take to get to that condition. Knowing this will help you judge whether it will be worth the cost of the repairs needed. Keep in mind it is rare for a restoration to come in under budget and more common to come in over budget. No matter what you think a restoration will cost, add at least 20 to 30 percent to it.

Cost versus resale value is an important concept to understand in order to avoid the trap of spending more to fix a boat up than it will ultimately be worth. Just because you spent $10,000 on restoring a boat does not mean it will be worth $10,000 more than when you bought it. I have seen many fall into this trap and be disappointed and out a lot of money in the end. There are many factors that affect the value of a boat and general condition is only one of them. Probably the biggest factors in determining a boat's value or potential value are age and brand, or class of boat. Even if your

▲ Interesting, but not likely to be easy to sell.

boat is in Bristol condition it will only be at the top of its value for that particular make and model of boat. Let's say you are looking at a thirty-foot powerboat. The average listing price for this model and year may be around $30,000. A boat of this type, even in very good condition, might sell for $50,000. This means that if you get the boat for $20,000 you really can only spend $20,000 to $30,000 on renovations before you start getting upside down, or dare I say, underwater in it. It is important to keep this in mind when selecting a good candidate for a project boat and setting up your budget.

I often hear from owners that it does not matter how much is spent on the boat since they don't plan to ever sell it. This may indeed be their plan but we all know life has a way of throwing curveballs at us and things can change. As mentioned earlier, heath, jobs, and family can and often do affect and change our plans. Also keep in mind a project boat that is not finished will always just be an unfinished project boat and its value will be low. Even if $20,000 in materials and parts have been purchased, the truth is they add little to the value until the boat is finished and usable. Even with new engines installed, if the interior is in pieces the boat will still have a low value and the expense of the new motors may be worth little in the resale value of the boat. This concept may be a hard pill to swallow for some but all one has to do is watch the eBay listings of project boats to see this is a valid point. Any project in pieces is not usable and often hard to transport. If a boat cannot easily be moved its value is less. Since there is a limited market for project boats, fewer buyers means lower value.

Of course, understanding the concept of a boat's value works both ways; it will help you spot the real jewel in the rough as well as the ones to avoid. Often a good boat can be found that may not show well but is basically in good condition and may only need a fair amount of elbow grease to get her back in shipshape. I have also seen many project boats where the seller has spent a fair amount on parts and materials but has never gotten around to putting it all together. This type of boat could be a good investment as well. As mentioned, the value will still be low due to the restoration being unfinished, but you will save money on buying many of the parts needed to complete the project.

Most project boats come in one of two categories, insurance salvage and neglected or abandoned boats. Insurance salvage boats are usually boats that were in service when they suffered some type of accidental loss that the insurance company felt would cost more to fix than the boat was insured for. The repair estimates really only have to come to around 75 percent of insured value for insurance companies to declare it a total loss. They know what I have stated, that repair costs almost always go over estimates so rather than get caught up in cost overruns, they simply pay the owner off and sell the boat for whatever they can get. Very often the owner buys the boat back from the insurance company and takes on the repairs themselves. They then use the insurance payout to fund the repairs.

▲ Is she worth saving?

Other times, the boat is sold through an open or closed auction. Insurance salvage boats can be good deal or a not-so-good deal depending on their pre-loss condition and the type of loss.

When considering an insurance salvage boat, it is important to try to assess the pre-loss condition. Keep in mind many insurance boats were in pretty poor shape to start with. Ignore the damage and look at the boat as if you were buying a used boat. Was it well cared for with recent maintenance and upgrades or was it an older, neglected boat that needed a lot of work prior to the loss? This is key to understanding the extent and scope of any repairs beyond just fixing the damage. You do not want to end up fixing the damage only to have to turn around and do a full restoration on the rest of the boat. This would end up being a bit of a "double jeopardy" so to speak.

It helps to understand what type of damage has occurred and what is involved in the repairs. Generally speaking, I try to avoid submerged boats unless they have been raised quickly and have been properly dried and preserved afterwards. Submersion is often partial but in some cases is total, so try to find out just how far she went down, how fast she was raised, and what was done to minimize damage. This may take a bit of detective work but will be worth the effort. Try to talk to the salvagers and anyone that might have firsthand knowledge of the loss. Try to get a hold of photos taken of the boat both prior to raising and just after. The more information you have the better. When inspecting it, pay close attention to waterlines inside lockers and other areas that might not have been fully cleaned up. Keep in mind any electronics and electrical equipment will almost always be ruined; this can also include wiring harnesses. Woodwork and cabinetry are often damaged as well; they may look fine on the surface but problems can emerge later as things dry out. Engines can sometimes be saved but anything electrical on the motors will have to be replaced or rebuilt. I have seen some motors where the cost to replace computers and other electronic controls came close to or exceeded the cost of a replacement motor. Do your research before placing that bid.

▲ Dock rash waiting to be fixed.

Another common type of loss is damage as a result of a collision. This includes collisions with other boats, a dock, other fixed structure, or the ground as in a hard grounding or beaching. Basically hitting anything hard and immovable that damages the boat. This may or may not result in holes in the boat and structural damage beyond what is at first visible. Sometimes this damage may be localized and limited but keep in mind boats are somewhat flexible and an impact in one area can cause damage to another area not even close to the original impact area. Some damage may appear to be superficial but requires a lot of work to access for repair. When inspecting impact damage, think long and hard about how the repairs will be made. If the repair looks easy and it is an insurance salvage, keep in mind the insurance company has hired professionals to assess the damage and they determined that it was going to cost close to the boat's insured value to repair. This may just be because they got high quotes from an expensive yard or it could be because they know something that is not obvious on casual inspection. There may also be water damage involved if the boat was grounded or the damage is below the waterline. If there is a hole above the waterline, there could be water damage from rain as well.

Fire damage is another common form of damage that causes insurance loss. Fire damage is often fairly comprehensive so care needs to be used when looking at one of these boats. Unless the fire was extinguished quickly or was from a fire outside of the boat, it often causes significant damage. If a fire starts in a cabin or enclosed space the heat is trapped and it quickly causes extensive damage. Fiberglass can be adversely affected by the extreme temperatures. It may appear okay on the surface but be severely damaged internally. Even a small fire can cause extensive smoke and heat damage. There can also be damage that resulted from extinguishing the fire. Water damage from fire hoses along with damage done while accessing the fire can add to it. Firemen do not carry axes because they look cool; it often takes brute force to get to where the fire is burning. Even a small fire extinguished with portable dry chemical extinguishers can have hidden damage. The chemicals used in this type of extinguisher are acidic and if not cleaned up quickly can cause problems, particularly to electrical components. Another problem with fire-damaged boats is getting rid of the residual odor left from burning plastics. This odor can linger for years even if the boat is well cleaned. This may make it unpleasant to be aboard and could affect the resale value of the boat. Fire damage from exterior sources tend to cause less damage but care still needs to be used for hidden damage from high temperatures. Exterior damage is generally easier to repair but the final finish can get expensive since the entire boat may need to be painted to make all the repairs match the existing finish.

Boat theft is on the rise and this could be another source for a project boat. I am not suggesting that you buy a boat from a guy who knows a guy in the parking lot of a big box store but boats

▲ Fire damage.

recovered from theft can be found at insurance and even police auctions. Generally speaking, they will be smaller, trailerable boats but sometimes larger vessels from theft loss can be found. These boats are often recovered intact after the insurance companies have paid the claim and other times they are recovered but damaged or stripped. The damage is often superficial but can include more severe collision and submersion damage. The full extent of any damage may not always be known, so care needs to be taken when evaluating the boat. Some thieves take a boat solely for the gear and equipment on it. Electronics, fishing gear, and outboards are at the top of the list. Thieves can do extensive and costly damage when trying to quickly remove gear. Tools of choice are often bolt cutters and sawzalls. I have seen transoms cut out or completely off in order to quickly get an outboard off. Electronics are simply cut free, often damaging wiring harnesses and dashboards in the process. Gear bolted to the deck is usually cut out, leaving gaping holes. Repairs can prove tricky, but not impossible.

Lightning and rig damage do not often result in a total loss but it does happen. The big problem with lightning is that the damage cannot always be easily seen. I have seen hulls turned to Swiss cheese as a result of lightning exiting through the copper bottom paint. There is often hidden damage to rigging as well as the electrical systems, which should be thoroughly checked. Rig damage in a sailboat is generally easy to fix but parts can be expensive. The loss has to be extensive for an insurance company to total a boat that has suffered rig damage. That said, masts and rigging are expensive so it does sometimes happen. This type of loss can make for a good project boat because it is often easy to repair. That said, if a rig has collapsed onto the deck there could also be structural and cosmetic damage that can add to the cost and workload. Special care needs to be used with any sailboat having a carbon fiber mast as these can be damaged by the lightning.

A final consideration with salvage boats is secondary damage caused by the salvage operation itself. Salvage crews have a job to do and although most will try to minimize damage, it is often hard to avoid. Most of the time this damage is limited, but I have seen rudders ripped off, rigs damaged, and new holes put in the boat. The stress placed on the structure during moving or lifting can cause hidden damage as well. Keels can be stressed causing internal damage not easily sighted. If a boat has been partially submerged, water can shift as the boat is righted, submerging sections and equipment that were once dry. It is important to keep this in mind when looking at a salvaged boat.

Then there are the neglected boats. There are plenty of older used boats out there sitting around just waiting for a new owner to bring them back to their former glory. Although these may seem like a great deal, they can easily turn into money pits. While a boat is sitting around unused, rubber deteriorates, fuel goes bad, wood rots, and critters and/or bugs can take up residence, causing even more

▲ Rudder damage due to recovery.

damage. That does not mean neglected boats are all a bad deal but you must be careful. The trick is to find a boat that was well kept and then let go for a short, recent period of time rather than a boat that has simply been poorly cared for its whole life. You can often find some real bargains with a neglected boat but not all owners have a realistic view of what their boat is worth. More times than not, I have found these owners think their boat is worth far more than it actually is. They have in mind what they have spent on the boat and do not see all the work that needs to be done. These owners think she will be good as new with just a little cleaning up but it usually takes more than just a bit of scrubbing and wax.

Beyond problems with unused equipment, neglected boats tend to have problems with rot and water damage, particularly from fresh water. Deck leaks tend to go unrepaired and often unnoticed in these boats. Fresh water can cause a lot of damage even in small quantities as it is a perfect medium for bacteria, fungus, mold, and other nasty things to grow in. This can quickly rot and damage woodwork. It can also damage structural wood in cored decks, hulls, and stringers. If looking at a neglected boat, pay particular attention for leaks. Look around windows, portlights, and hatches as well as other deck fittings. Look for signs of leaks and water damage inside the boat. For sailboats, pay extra attention to mast steps, supports, and chainplate attachments as these can suffer water damage resulting in rot, rust, and corrosion. On outboard boats the transom and stringers tend to be problem areas due to rot in wood under the fiberglass. These all can be expensive to repair.

Boats stored on land for long periods of time can have their own unique problems. Boats are designed and built to be supported by water. Although most are fine sitting on land for several months, many have problems when on land for several years. Even fiberglass can sag and change shape when left improperly supported for long periods of time. Jack stands and supports can cause dents or

▲ She's been out for awhile.

depressions in the hull, keels can be damaged, and rainwater can all add to the problems. Rainwater is perhaps the biggest issue as it can add weight to the boat, freeze and expand in the winter, and cause rot. Dirt and leaves often cause drains and scuppers to clog, allowing rainwater to accumulate. An advantage to a boat stored on land is it might be easier to move or work on. You can also have a chance to fully inspect the bottom. Boats left unmaintained in the water can have damage from marine growth and galvanic corrosion that cannot be detected without hauling.

Whether the boat is in the water or out, any boat left unused is likely to have some form of insect or rodent infestation. This can be anything from a few wasps to rats living in it. Insects can bore holes in wood and clog vents and hoses. I have seen vent fittings completely clogged by spider nests, causing all sorts of problems, including collapsed tanks. Rats and other rodents can cause extensive damage to wiring and hoses as well as cushions and sails. Try to keep an eye out for signs of trouble when looking at a neglected boat. Rodent droppings, signs of nesting, holes, and the like will all be clues you should look for. Care should be used when boarding and inspecting a neglected boat. It is a good idea to open lockers cautiously and carry some wasp spray with you.

Bankruptcy and estate sales can make good project boat candidates as well. During economic downturns there is usually a healthy market for bankruptcy boats. Even when times are good there is usually a steady supply of boats being liquidated by banks. The problem with these boats is that they can be neglected and some owners will strip the boat clean of anything of value. Banks generally do not want to hold a boat for very long. They know the longer they own it, the less the boat will be worth and it will cost more for storage and upkeep, so you could say they are motivated sellers. Of course, banks still want their money back so will try and get as much as they can. Estate sales can be hard to find as they are not normally listed as such. Dock masters tend to be a good source of information with these boats as they often know the owners and family. Dealing with families can be tricky, though. Some may be anxious to sell while others may have a misguided idea of the value of their loved one's pride and joy. Often, estate boats have sat unused for some time, so as with neglected boats care needs to be taken. The wealthier the owner and family, the better the condition is likely to be.

Then there are the abandoned or derelict boats. These can be found in the back lots of many boatyards and sometimes anchored in back coves. If the boat is on the hard in a boatyard, you might be able to buy it from the boatyard as they can claim ownership for back storage fees. Often the yard will sell the boat cheap just to get rid of it or to collect at least some back storage fees. Make sure you are able to get all the proper paperwork and clear title to the boat. The boatyard has to first go through the process of taking ownership and getting the title. When it comes to derelict boats out in a back cove, things are a bit trickier. Obtaining ownership and proper titles can

▲ This one is going to need a lot of work.

be very difficult and can often take years to do. It would not be wise to put any money into a derelict boat until you have proper title and ownership. With either derelict or abandoned boats you also want to make sure there are no liens or back taxes owed on it. If you are not careful, you could find yourself owing more than the boat is worth.

So where should you start looking for a project boat? It's best to begin close to home. After all, transportation costs for any boat more than forty or fifty miles away from you immediately increases the cost depending on the size. If you are looking for a small boat that can be trailered this may not be an issue. If the boat has its own trailer just make sure it is road-worthy before hitting the highway. The cost of transporting larger boats can add up fast. If you have to hire a transportation company, keep in mind there might be loading and unloading costs at each end. Water transportation can be an option but only if the boat has enough working systems that it can safely be moved. Do not take the seller's word that "it just needs a new battery," find out for yourself its full condition before heading out to sea.

Knowing what type of boat you are looking for will also direct where to start your search. For larger boats, local marinas and boatyards are always a good place to start. Walking the docks and back lots can be fun and you never know what gem you might find. With smaller boats, you just might find what you are looking for in someone's backyard so keep an eye out when driving around town. There are also many outboard dealers located away from the water that may have that center console you are looking for. As you travel about, ask around and see if anyone knows of any good deals. You never know what you might find. Many times, the best deals come from a guy who knows a guy. You just have to follow the thread, at the end could be your perfect boat.

Although most boat brokers are not really interested in dealing with project boats, it could be worth a few calls as they may know of some possibilities out there. After all, it is their job to know what is on the market even if they are not listing it. Craigslist is also a good place

▲ A little pricey for a project.

to look along with any other local online sales sites or print listings. Contact your local insurance and salvage/tow boat companies to see if they know of any insurance salvage boats for sale. They usually know of boats that may soon be listed and some salvagers even handle sales for insurance companies. Local marine surveyors can also be good to talk to as some handle insurance claims and most know what yards might be the best to look at. If you cannot find anything to suit your needs close to home, expand your search area a bit while still staying somewhat close. When looking for insurance boats you can try the insurance companies themselves, but it can be hard to get much information from them. Most have better things to do than talk to yet another bargain hunter. However, they may give you some information on auction houses and other liquidators.

If there is nothing close to where you live that fits what you are looking for, you can broaden your search to national outlets. EBay should be on the top of the list of places to look. There is always a steady supply of used boats of all types listed. EBay is also very safe as their buyer protection services favor the buyer. If you do buy a boat through eBay you can place a deposit on the boat before looking at it. If things are not what you were expecting, PayPal will refund the deposit in most cases. As mentioned, there are some auction companies that handle sales for insurance companies. These companies can be very good to work with and can help with the logistics of getting the boat to you. Most have websites with listings of what they have in inventory at any given time and many will list upcoming auctions as well.

Often the best deals are made when you spot a boat in a marina and follow up by talking to the management and making the calls needed to track down the owner. This, of course, requires getting out and exploring marinas and boatyards, taking notes, and making lots of phone calls. You might encounter a lot of rejection by using this method as many owners will resent someone asking if their boat is for sale just because it looks like it has not been used in ten years. Others will simply think their boat is worth what it was when it was new. It is best to just move on from these owners. But every now and then you just may find a willing seller who just wants to get rid of the boat. For larger boats you may be able to look up the owner from the US Coast Guard documentation search using the vessel name.

Once a potential boat of interest has been located, the first thing you should do is to research it. Make sure it will fit your needs and maybe get a bit of history to know its strong and weak points. There are many online forums to help you learn about a particular make and model of boat. Then do some valuations to know just what a completed boat is worth. Look for boats of the same model and year to give you an idea of average sales prices. Finally, do some guesstimating on repair costs. Remember, it is better to overestimate than to underestimate. Keep in mind engine hours, equipment lists, as well as overall condition when estimating value. Think about any costs in transporting the boat as well. If all the numbers look good and you like the boat, it may be time to pull the trigger.

For a boat that is being auctioned there are a few strategies that will help ensure a good deal. First, know your top price. The biggest mistake many make is not setting a top price before starting the bidding or not sticking to it. If you have done your homework this should be a relatively easy number to come up with. Keep in mind it is easy to get caught up in the competition of bidding, but if you have a top price and stick to it you will not get in over your head. There are basically two types of auctions, open and closed bidding. Open bidding is where you know what the other guy is bidding, closed is one where you have no clue what others have bid and you submit your best bid and hope it is a winning one. EBay is a bit of a hybrid in that you may know the other guy's bid but you do not know his auto bid number. It may help to bid in slightly odd numbers like $78.78 instead of $75.50. The reason is most people bid in even amounts so you could win by just a few dollars or even a few cents more than someone you are bidding against. With many online auctions such as eBay, there are often a lot of bids placed in the last minutes of the auction. This is another reason to have a top price and stick to it. No deal is so good you cannot walk away from it. Be sure you understand all the auction rules before bidding as well. There may be time limits on when the boat has to be moved and there can be additional fees for processing paperwork and such. Understand the fine print before placing that bid. Some auction companies may also require a deposit or a credit check prior to bidding. Payment is often due shortly after the auction ends and it may have to be in the form of a certified check or wire transfer. It would be a shame to win and find your bid was disqualified because of a technicality so understand the rules from the beginning.

When shopping used boats that are actively for sale where the seller is known, it just becomes a matter of making an offer once you are sure the boat is what you are looking for. As with a boat being auctioned, you have to do your homework ahead of time to know

4 Now What?

You have finally done it and gotten your new (at least new to you) boat. The boat is safely located where you will be working on it and you're ready to get started. Chisels are sharpened, new blades in the saws, extension cords carefully run, it is time to get to work! But where do you start? It is at this point that many people make the single biggest mistake of all, one that often dooms the project to failure from the very beginning. So put down those tools and let's talk about how best to proceed.

The single biggest mistake many people make when starting a project boat is gutting it. I am not sure why so many feel that they need to start by completely taking the boat apart but this is often a serious mistake. There are several reasons you should not do this. The first is that once you have taken the boat apart it essentially becomes worthless. Should you for some reason need to sell the boat, it will be difficult at best to do so after it is taken apart. Nobody wants to buy a project boat in a million pieces, and in many cases it would be difficult to even give it away. Another reason you do not want to do this is that by doing so you increase the amount of work needed to get the boat back to usable condition. By gutting the boat you may compromise the structural integrity of the hull as well. There are good reasons boats are built the way they are and unless you have a really thorough understanding of marine engineering you could be affecting the strength of your boat as a whole. Finally, keeping track of all the pieces becomes a challenge and it is likely key parts will become lost.

I have only seen a few project boats that once gutted were successfully put back together; most end up sitting around for years in pieces with the owners overwhelmed by the work ahead of them. It is always easier to take something apart than to put it back together.

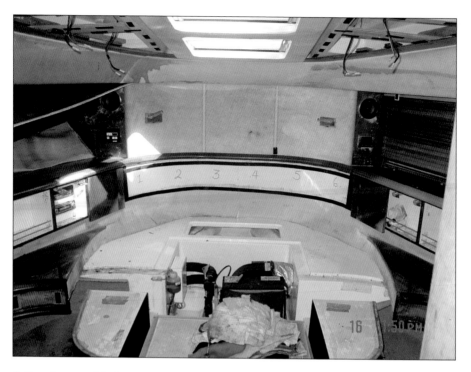

▲ Removing parts of the interior.

Unless you have a lot of time and some real boat-building skills, gutting a boat makes little sense. Granted there are a few cases where this should be done, but in most cases it is best to take things one step at a time. If you absolutely have to change how the boat is laid out it is still best to take it in small steps. There may be some cases where taking things apart to get to structural problems is required, but even then I suggest you take no more apart then is absolutely necessary.

There is also a temptation at this point to redesign the boat and do things the way you want them. This may seem like a good idea but, once again, unless you are really skilled or have boat-building experience this seldom proves to be a good idea. There are many things that need to be taken into consideration when doing a redesign; weights and the vessel structure are among the most important. I have seen more than one project boat where the owner redesigned the boat to make it "better" only to find it no longer floated correctly on its lines, listed to one side, or worse, sank upon launching. If you must redesign the boat, either make sure you know what you are doing or get professional help from a marine designer or engineer. Also keep in mind that resale value will be compromised with major changes. Most boats are designed to appeal to a broad market. If highly customized, it will have a much narrower market and therefore not have the same resale value. The only exception to this may be with a custom-built or home-built boat that that may not have a value based on design and could be improved with some redesign. Think carefully before you start doing a complete redesign, though. You can often get the same results with small or non-permanent changes.

So where do you start? There is no simple answer. No two project boats are alike so each requires their own approach. I generally recommend starting by bringing the boat back to or close to original condition. Only then should you start to think about making modifications. By doing this, you will protect your investment and

▲ Making your work list.

help with resale value should you need to sell the boat prior to completion. By focusing on returning the boat to near original shape will also get the boat back to a usable condition sooner, allowing you to use the boat before moving on to customizing. I think it is important to be able to use your project boat for more than just working on. It can help your morale to be able to take your project boat out and get some pleasure from it as you work on it. This will also help you understand what changes, if any, make the most sense as you proceed.

The first tools to get out are a pen, a notepad, and a digital camera. I realize you are anxious to get started but the best thing to do is take some time with your new project and get a good understanding of what really needs to be done. If you have not had a survey this may be a good time to hire a surveyor to at least help and look things over with you. There are a couple of good reasons to get someone from outside to help. First, any decent surveyor is trained to spot trouble areas; they should have the proper equipment to find things you may have missed. Surveyors will have an independent eye, meaning they are looking at the boat differently than you will because let's face it, they don't have a dime in her. A good surveyor can advise you on safety standards and can help make sure you do not end up doing things twice. Finally, you are going to need insurance and you will most likely need a survey for this. If you have someone who has worked with you throughout the project, they can help update things as you go to make sure your insurance properly covers your investment.

The planning you do at this point can save time and money in the long run so take your time. Make a list of all the repairs needed to just get the boat back up and running. Skip the modifications for now; we will get back to that later. Do not worry about priorities; just put together a full list of everything that needs to be fixed, big and small. Take pictures of items that need work for future reference. Photos can be helpful for planning as well as identifying parts and problem areas. Photos will also be fun to look back on as you proceed so you can see how much has really been accomplished.

With a list of needed repairs in hand you can now prioritize where you need to start. On the top of the list should be things that will help stabilize and protect the boat from further damage. Identify anything that may cause damage to the boat due to weather or other hazards such as sinking or fire. If the boat is not covered, deck leaks that will damage the interior or deck coring should be addressed right away. You will want to make sure the boat is properly blocked and supported. Poor supports can cause more damage to the structure so this is important. Never block a boat on soft ground and make sure there is no loose, dry brush nearby that could be a fire hazard. Keeping rainwater out of the boat is important when on land. If the boat does not already have a bilge drain to allow rain water to escape, you may want to add one. Make sure deck drains and scuppers are clear and remain that way. I have seen many a good boat damaged by a clogged drain. This is particularly true if there are trees that can

▲ Getting to work.

drop leaves nearby. It is surprising how quickly a few leaves will clog a scupper or drain.

For boats in the water, thru-hulls and below waterline fittings are both important. I have seen more than one project boat sink at the slip because the owner was more interested in a new paint job than replacing a bad hose. As with land-based boats, you will want to take care of any deck leaks, which can cause a surprising amount of damage in a short time. Make sure the bilge pumps are in good working order and that the bilges are clean and free of debris that could clog the pumps. Check that the boat is properly secured and that the dock lines and cleats are in good condition. Just because it is a project does not mean you should skimp on dock lines and fenders. You do not want to end up doing more work because a line chafed through.

Once the boat is in stable condition, it is time to think about getting set up to get to work. This is the time to put up things like ladders and

▲ Ramping up. *Photo by Banks Chamberlin.*

scaffolds, install tarps or covers, and in general get everything ready to make the work easier and safer. Don't get carried away, just keep it simple and do only what needs to be done when it needs to be done. You don't want to start off spending time and money on fancy covers and such that may not be needed in the long run. Focus on safety and protecting the boat without getting too elaborate.

It is now time to think about getting your work list prioritized. I always try to do things in my head first, sort of virtual planning. I try to visualize how things will be done and mentally go through each process. This helps me spot problems and think about how one project might affect another. You do not want to paint the cockpit if you still have to pull the motor out and you would not want to refinish the interior if you have to remove a fuel tank. Some of this may seem obvious but by thinking things through you can save yourself a lot of extra work. Write down the order of work while thinking of parallel projects that can be done at the same time.

Planning the workflow requires a bit of creativity as well. I have found it often helps to have several jobs or tasks in process all at once. This way, should you be held up on any particular task you can just move on to another task without losing too much momentum. It also allows time to source parts that are not immediately available. Any time you are working on a project boat it can be expected that you will run into problems and roadblocks to progress. It helps to allow for this and expect these to occur; not doing so will lead to frustration and disappointment. The trick is to find ways to work around these problems. I once had a manager who always said, "There are no problems, only opportunities." I got where he was coming from although I have to admit some of these "opportunities" were often more troublesome than rewarding. To this day when a problem occurs I try not to get upset and simply say, "Well, there is another opportunity to fix!"

When planning the work, plan for "opportunities" and leave extra time in your schedule in the event that something goes wrong. This will help avoid frustration and keep the work moving. Try to find a few projects to set aside that are not time-critical but can be used as filler projects when having to wait for parts and such on the main project. For example, if you need to do some refinishing of small parts, set them aside to work on should you need to wait for, say, parts for the engine. Or do some rigging or electrical work while waiting for fiberglass or paint to cure. By having a few tasks like this set aside as filler work, you can maintain a consistency of workflow and get more done.

It is also important to plan for weather. If you live in an area with a seasonal climate this is particularly important. Unless you are lucky enough to have your project inside a climate-controlled space, it will be important to plan for the winter cold and summer heat. Certain tasks simply cannot be done if the temperatures are too extreme and others are just not practical to do if conditions are harsh. Keep this in mind when planning the workflow. Plan to have tasks set aside for rainy days, and you can do inside work during the winter and outside work during the summer. This may seem obvious but can easily be overlooked.

▲ The old has to come out first.

It is generally best to start off with the major repairs that will require taking things apart. Bad deck core or rotten bulkheads or floors should be done first. Next would come any major mechanical and electrical projects. Start inside and work your way out, if possible. Do the dirty work first and then move on to the fancy stuff. If the boat has a cabin, start on the inside because any work done there is not subject to weathering and will not need as much maintenance as you proceed. If engines or major equipment need service or removal this is a good place to start as well. I recall one owner I knew who gutted the interior then proceeded to spend weeks on a high-end exterior paint job. Once he finished the exterior paint, he moved back to the inside which took a couple of years. In the process, the deck paint was damaged by walking on it and weathering and he ended up drilling holes through the new finish. When all was said and done he had to do the paint job all over again. Careful planning will avoid doing things twice.

Once again, avoid the temptation to just go in and tear things out. Things are often not as bad as they may look on the surface. I have done electrical work on more than one boat where the wiring looked like a complete mess until I cleared away the top layer of aftermarket, owner-installed wiring. Under the mess was the boat's original wiring which was still in good condition. Had I just ripped it all haphazardly out I would have had to do a lot more work. Go slowly and only remove what you have to and do not be afraid to stop and think things over before proceeding. That said, there are times when it is better to remove things that may not necessarily require removal. An example of this might be to remove a motor in order to be able to fully access an engine compartment for cleaning and repainting. This is where that mental preparation will help; visualize the process one step at a time before proceeding. Think about how to get around problem areas.

This is also the time to think about sourcing parts and supplies, particularly larger items. Think about the order of work and what will be needed and when. It makes little sense to buy items like electronics and life rafts when just getting started; they will often be outdated by the time you get to using them. The only reasons to purchase something not needed right away is when you can get a really good deal and the part will not become dated, or it's a hard-to-find part that you know will be needed at some point and you are not likely to find a good source for it in the future. The trick is to focus only on what is critical to getting your project boat back up and running. You can always add the toys and fun stuff later. Remember, cost overruns are inevitable. It is important to start saving early by being conservative and not spending more than you need to from the start.

There are some parts that may take time to source—hard to find items such as good used motors, masts, replacement OEM parts, and so on. You should keep an eye out for anything that is no longer available or very expensive to source new and be ready to purchase should you find a good deal. One boat I restored had a damaged aluminum toe rail that was no longer made. It would have cost a

▲ Keeping track of things.

couple of thousand dollars to replace with a new one. It took a year and a half of searching but I was able to locate an exact replacement for a few hundred dollars. This did not slow down the project since there were other things I was working on during this time. My patience saved me money that I was later able to put into more fun things like new electronics.

Making a list of all the major parts you will need along with a timeline for when they will be needed will allow you to get the best deals. It will also help avoid wasting money on things that look like a good deal but may not really be needed. The process of sourcing parts can take a long time, but if done right can also save thousands of dollars in the end. Keep in mind it helps to be creative and knowing what is needed will keep you focused.

As the work proceeds it helps to update your plans and workflow. It is hard to predict all the problems (or opportunities) that may arise while working on the boat. You are likely to run into unexpected issues and things you did not expect to have to repair. Leave room in your schedule and budget for this. It is pretty common knowledge that everything takes longer than expected so leaving room in your schedule will help avoid frustration. Be flexible in how you plan your work and be prepared to adjust as needed.

I have found that breaking each task down into smaller tasks helps to get things moving. Instead of looking at the big picture, look at all the little ones that make up the whole task. For example, you may need to remove a motor. This is easy to break down into smaller steps. Start by setting up, getting the tools ready, and adding protection to the boat as needed. Next, drain the fluids and so on. Breaking your projects down like this will make them more manageable and less daunting.

Another aspect of planning the work is providing for help and outside labor. Few people can be expected to be able to do all the work themselves so you will probably need to hire outside help. This may be just requiring manual labor or, more likely, skilled craftsmen to do specific tasks. You may need to hire a mechanic to help repair

▲ Sometimes you need help.

a motor, a canvas person to replace a worn Bimini, or an electrician to help with wiring. Good planning here can also save money. These craftsmen tend to be very busy in season and slow out of season. With proper planning you can use this to your advantage by hiring them during slow times for a slightly better rate. The trick is to plan and have everything ready for them when the slow season starts. It also pays to talk to them ahead of time so that they may be able to let you know what they may need from you to get things done. This may not always be possible as in the case of painters and fiberglass work. These tasks need to be done when the weather permits, but contacting the craftsmen early and planning ahead for when they will be needed can save time and money.

While I realize I said you should focus on returning the boat to a stock usable condition, there will be some future upgrades you may want to think about as you proceed. If your goal is to keep the boat and use it for your own personal use you may want to think about preparing for this while doing the restoration work. Say you plan on installing a windlass at some point; if you are in in the process of doing electrical work it may make sense to go ahead and run the wires and set the panel up for this. If you are upgrading the electrical panel, it would not hurt to install the breakers needed for any new equipment or electronics you plan to add. This type of planning for upgrades doesn't add a lot to the overall cost of the restoration and will make future upgrades easier. It could actually even add to the value should you have to sell before you are completely finished. A new owner is likely to want at least some of the upgrades you had planned.

Another thing to think about is planning your free time to do the boat work. This may not be a problem if you are retired, but many of us need to keep working our day jobs to earn our boat bucks. Good

▲ Halfway there.

planning from the start will help keep things moving at a steady pace. Some folks get themselves into trouble by failing to set up a regular schedule to work on their boat. If the time needed to do the work is not properly planned for and set aside it becomes all too easy to start putting things off and as time goes on the work slows down.

Many start off with great enthusiasm and work many hours only to lose steam as the project proceeds. It is important to leave time for family and friends as well as some to time relax and recharge. If all you are doing is boat work, you will soon lose enthusiasm and may even find those close to you will start to resent the time spent on the boat and not with them. Remember, this is a long race and you have to be like the tortoise and keep going at a steady pace if you are to succeed. Thinking about this from the start will help keep everything moving along at a good rate and avoid future burnout on the project. Remember, this should be a fun, positive experience, not a hard-fought sprint to the end.

Getting a good start and setting the flow early will assure the project will proceed to a smooth finish. What you do at the start can often set the tone for the rest of the project. Do not dig a deep hole at the start by taking on more than needs to be done. Plan the work carefully and stick to your plan as much as you can. Some adjustments will be needed along the way but do not allow yourself to get too far off the rails and get sucked into side projects and things that are not important. This is why even a simple plan is critical. I like to keep a notebook where I outline the plan, making changes as needed and adding sub-plans to break things down into manageable parts. I find it helps to be able to write things down at the work site and then reorganize the big plan as needed.

What you do at the very beginning can make or break the whole project. Think long and hard before you get that crowbar out and start taking things apart. Do the big things and systems first and save the painting until the end. Plan carefully and try not to do more than is needed. All this will help ensure success.

5 Eating Elephants

Most of us have heard the expression, "If you have to eat an elephant, do it one bite at a time." Think of your boat restoration as an elephant served up and ready for your consumption. It simply cannot be done all at once so eating it one bite at a time is exactly how you should approach it. Any boat restoration is a series of small steps leading to the final result of a finished boat ready to set to sea. By breaking a larger project or beast down into ever smaller steps, each becomes a bit more manageable. Keeping this in mind will help with planning and execution and will help keep the project from seeming too overwhelming.

With every project boat I have ever tackled there is always that moment when I first get the boat and sit there wondering, *WTF have I gotten myself into?* This usually does not last too long before the planner in me kicks in and I begin to mentally dissect the project. I begin to think about all the big and little tasks needed to complete it. I break things down in my mind into ever smaller parts until I get to the point of getting off my butt and getting the tools out (or the fork and knife, so to speak). Every big meal starts with the first bite. I find it helps to imagine myself doing the work and thinking about all the small steps it takes to reach the end goal. For me, this is part of the fun of restoring a boat, imagining what can be. After all, being able to see the potential is why many of us get project boats in the first place.

Even a small restoration can be a bit intimidating when looking at the entire project as a whole, sort of like sitting down to dinner and seeing a whole elephant on the table, wondering just how you are going to eat it! For this reason, I have found it to be better to break the project down into smaller steps or pieces and focus on completing those smaller bits one at a time without getting too overwhelmed. Breaking the big project down into manageable steps is critical to

▲ A potential project.

success and an important part of any plan. To use yet another cliché, every journey begins with the first step. This is also true of any boat restoration. A good project plan will start with the big chunks and keep breaking them down into ever smaller pieces. Only by doing this will it become clear where to start and how to proceed.

Every project needs a starting point. Getting off on the wrong foot can set a project back from the beginning so it is important to set your plan up to find the right starting point. A good plan starts with the completed project and works backwards to picking up that first tool. It will also help define how all the smaller tasks fit together. Clearly some things will need to be completed before others can start. It makes little sense to start painting a deck if the core needs repair. On the other hand, painting the deck before installing the hardware would make sense. Being able to see all of the tasks at once will help plan the order in which they need to be done. Knowing all the little tasks to be done will in the end help select the best starting place and it may not be what you first thought.

Even a small project needs some sort of plan, even a simple one. A plan can be as basic as a notebook with the tasks and subtasks or a bit more sophisticated as in a computer spreadsheet. For any project taking more than a week or so I like to use a spreadsheet. Anyone with basic computer skills can master working with a spreadsheet program. One of the nice things about spreadsheets is they allow for rapid changes and updates, automatically adjusting totals so it is always clear where the overall project stands. After all, it important to know just how much of the elephant is left to eat.

Every plan needs to be broken down into ever smaller steps in order to accomplish the end result. Clearly, you will not be able to do everything all at once. This was driven home to me when I was taking a robotics class several years ago. Our team had decided to program a robotic arm to make breakfast. This seemed like a relatively easy task on the surface. Simply tell the robot what to do, right? We quickly learned that not only are robots really stupid but they will also do just

▲ A robot making breakfast. *Courtesy of Vital Imagery Ltd.*

what you tell them to, right or wrong. You also have to tell them to do every little thing. Our team quickly learned each process had to be broken down into ever smaller tasks. Each step, from opening the gripper to moving in the needed direction, had to be programmed. Our goal was to have the robot cook an egg, make toast, and make a cup of coffee. This all seemed pretty simple; however, the total number of small steps to get there was enlightening to say the least.

So what does a breakfast-cooking robot have to do with restoring a boat and why is this important to how you plan your work? It clearly illustrates how everything starts and ends with small steps that add up to a finished meal ready to enjoy. This is a key concept to understand when working on any restoration. Keeping in mind that all big projects start and end with very small tasks is important to not only getting the work done but it can keep motivation and momentum going when needed.

▲ Making a plan.

It is the same way when planning a restoration. It is not enough to simply know you have to paint the deck. Painting starts with cleaning the deck, then sanding, then repairing damaged areas, then cleaning again, and so on until you get to the point of actually applying the paint, and even then you still have to remove masking tape and touch up. A good plan will take all this into consideration. Of course there is also a balance to be made in that breaking everything down into too many small steps will waste time. It takes a bit of experience to learn just how far to go when making the plan. Be practical and try to keep it as simple as possible without losing too much detail.

Back when I was building and repairing boats every job started with the plan; even small jobs had a simple plan. This plan was used to give estimates, set costs, and assign labor. It was updated as the project or job progressed. I would set up a simple spreadsheet to list all the tasks with their estimated costs adding columns to record actual costs and times. I could then compare and monitor each phase and task of the overall restoration. This spreadsheet does not have to be complicated as I tried to keep things as simple as possible while still providing the detail needed. Trust me, like many others I am not big on doing a lot of paperwork, but in the long run the time spent will be well worth the effort. Let's face it, most of us would rather be grinding fiberglass on a hot summer's day rather than doing paperwork but it is an important part of the job.

Setting up a project plan is not hard. For small simple projects you could just do this the old-fashioned way and keep handwritten notes in a notebook with some basic estimates for times to do the task along with simple parts lists. This is most useful for smaller projects or doing maintenance work. I keep a notebook on my own boat for doing the little jobs or when making small modifications. For bigger, more complex jobs, a computer spreadsheet is the way to go.

Pretty much everyone has a computer these days and most come equipped with at least one spreadsheet program. Microsoft Excel is

▲ Planning on the computer.

perhaps the most popular of these although it is not the only one available. Open Office is a free program available online that is very similar to MS Office. Google Sheets allows you to work online and save the work to your Google Drive or OneDrive. Keeping the file in the "cloud" makes it available from any location with Internet access. With this, the spreadsheet would be available at home, your office, or while on the job site. Having this information always available allows you to keep up to date in real time. Having a laptop or tablet would help, but most smartphones could be used as well. Using a computer spreadsheet may seem a bit intimidating to some, but the truth of the matter is they are generally not hard to use and, with a little practice, can even be fun to do. If you have not used a spreadsheet before start simple and add to it as your skills improve. The beauty of using a spreadsheet is its flexibility. It may be possible to find someone to set up a basic template for you which could then be modified as needed, and many templates can be found online to get you started. There are some project planning software packages out there but I have found most are simply too complicated for anything but the largest restorations.

When building a spreadsheet, I like to set up the first column for the tasks or jobs, followed by a column for estimated labor times, and another for estimated parts cost. After those I add columns for actual labor times and actual material costs for tracking and comparing. Totals are at the bottom so that I can keep track of the big picture. I then will add sub-tasks below each main task which, in turn, generate more detailed parts and labor lists. If things get too complicated on a single spreadsheet I will use small sub-spreadsheets for a more detailed view of each task, these can be linked to a main spreadsheet showing overall estimates and totals. There are different ways to set something like this up; whether using a computer or a simple notebook the point is to set up a realistic plan that can be tracked.

For some, a Gantt bar chart showing timelines for the work may be helpful, but personally I have not found them that useful and a bit complex to use. I prefer a simple calendar to plan what I will be doing and when I will do it. Personally, I have found a date book works well for me but everyone is different. As with spreadsheets, find what you are comfortable with and use that system. There are many resources online for templates ready to be customized for what works best for your way of doing things. I try not to push any single method of estimating and tracking as everyone is different and what works for one person may not work for another. The important thing is to have a plan and to track expenses and work as it proceeds. Many may find this tedious and a waste of time but if it is done correctly it will save time, money, and possibly rework. It is important to find a system you are comfortable with if you are to stick with it.

It is equally important to keep spreadsheets and plans up to date as the work proceeds. Even the best plans will soon be out of date once the work begins. We all know nothing ever takes as long or costs what we expect it to. Problems occur and tasks cost more or take longer than expected. There are also times, admittedly not as often, that tasks will go well and not be as hard or expensive as first thought. This is why it is important to stay current on any plans and budgets made. Many take the time to build the initial plan but then fail to keep up with it as work proceeds and things change. If not kept up with, the plan becomes out of date at some point and basically useless. Adjusting your plans as you go is important to keeping the project as a whole under control.

Even the best plans are useless if they are not maintained. You cannot just set up the spreadsheet, tack it to the wall, and forget it. A big part of project planning is project management. This is the part where you keep track of the plans and update them to meet the ever-changing circumstances. As work proceeds, it is inevitable that plans will change. Problems will be found requiring more work, some parts may not come in when you hoped, or the weather may suddenly change on you. Nothing is going to go exactly as planned but this is not a problem as long as you are prepared for it. I call this going around obstacles. When some people are faced with a problem they either try in vain to fight through it or worse yet,

▲ Tracking progress.

stop dead in their tracks. The real trick is to be able to dodge the problems as they arise.

Being able to track your progress and expenses will allow you to spot problem areas before they get out of control. By tracking progress in labor hours and material costs, it becomes possible to determine when things are costing more than planned. This information will allow you to adjust the work or cut back some to control costs. It is inevitable that some tasks will cost more than expected. At times this simply cannot be avoided, but knowing this it may be possible to curtail less important tasks to maintain the overall project expenses. This can only be done knowing where things stand compared to estimates. It is all too easy to lose track of what is going into a restoration without some method of tracking labor and expenses. A simple, well-maintained plan updated regularly will make tracking this possible.

It is good to have a few overlapping tasks set up as well. This way if you hit a problem on the main task there will be another task ready to work on. This will help avoid frustration and keep work moving efficiently. I have a rule that when I run into a problem that requires a part I do not have, I do not stop work to go get that part. Instead I note on a list the part needed and move on to another task that I can proceed with. The next time I am out getting parts or ordering parts online, I get what was needed. This way I do not waste time running around for parts or supplies. This applies to tools I may not have on hand as well. Of course there may be exceptions to this when something is critical to getting an important task done, but as a rule it is best to try to be as efficient as possible.

I usually have a few simple and non-critical filler tasks I keep ready to work on should I get hung up on my main task. Small jobs such as painting lockers, cleaning up, and other simple tasks all work well for filler projects. Anything that may not require a lot of special supplies and can take advantage of supplies always on hand work well. Let's face it, there are always a ton of little jobs that need doing. Keeping a list of these non-essential tasks will keep the work moving along if the main task of the day gets held up. Think of all these little tasks as the side dishes to the main meal. They may not be as important as the main dish but they add to the overall meal. It is often the little tasks that can slow a project down in the end so being able to get some done as the restoration proceeds will save time in the long run.

Keeping running lists is an important part of being efficient as well. The larger parts needed for a task will be in the written plan but it is impossible to predict every little part and tool needed for a given project. No matter how carefully you think things through, there will always be that part or tool you simply did not plan on that is needed to move forward. As I work I keep a notebook to jot down what is needed and reminders for tools and other supplies to bring to the job site the next time I am going there. Each evening when I get back from the boat I will load up the materials needed for the following day's work. On my way to the boat I will stop at the store and pick up the small parts as needed. I envy those that can just remember everything without a list but writing things down is the only way I can keep track

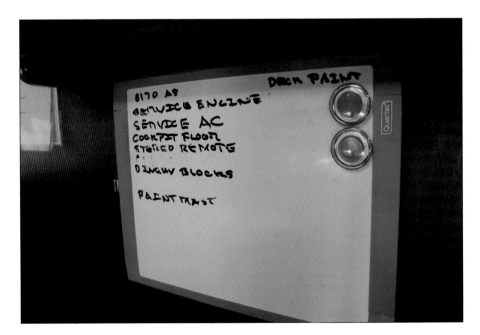

▲ Using a whiteboard for planning.

of what I need for the next day's work. I also find these lists handy to have should I need to look back to see what I did on a particular task. A notebook is also a good place to note dimensions of parts used. This can be helpful at a later date should something need replacing.

Having a dry-erase board to jot notes down in the work area is helpful for quick notes. I keep a list of tasks in process along with other notes about the job. I can write down important dimensions for items along with other useful information. This keeps all this information out where it is easy to find at a glance. The drawback is that once erased, the information is gone so I often transfer this information to written paper notes. If I am in a real hurry, I will snap a photo of the board with my cellphone for future reference. What I like about a dry-erase board is that it is easy to update and the information is readily available for anyone working with me. If you have people helping you, this is a great way to make sure you are all working from the same information.

Keeping jobs from getting too complicated is important. Many, myself included, tend to overcomplicate tasks while not meaning to. The trick is to stay within the plan and budget wherever possible. Think of it as being a bit like electricity trying to find the path of least resistance. There is no need to make each meal a full banquet when a simple picnic would do. Keeping tasks simple will help speed the project along and keep costs under control. This will often mean just trying to keep the boat as it was without getting too far into redesigning it. An old friend used the expression, "Honor the medium." By this, he meant try to maintain the same style and methods of doing things. I most often see this applied with woodwork projects whether being repaired or modified. Most do not take the time to study how the boat is built and the styles used. They instead do the work the way they think it should be done or in the style they like. This most often results in work that sticks out like a sore thumb and looks different from everything else. Even high quality work will not look "right" if it does not match the surrounding level of quality and style. Most production boats use some fairly simple construction

▲ Work in progress.

methods to keep costs down. By following the builder's lead and doing the repairs the same way as the boat was built will make work easier and faster in the long run as well as maintaining the original look. I have always said the best repair is the one you cannot tell was done, so be careful about "improving" things.

Many dockside "advisors" (or the other boat owner's with too much free time) will tell you that some work *has* to be done this way or that. Doing the work to a higher standard is fine as long as it doesn't take things to extremes and busts the budget. I always try to do electrical and plumbing at a high standard while trying to do the more showy things to the same style the boat was built in, keeping in mind the boat's use will dictate the level of quality followed. If your goal is to bring the boat back to original, such as when restoring an older classic, following the original manufacturer's methods is best. If restoring or outfitting for offshore or long-range cruising, keeping a high quality level is important. For most, following the builder's style will be sufficient and help maintain the boat's value. If you're going to make improvements, carefully select how and where they are done.

Leaving unfinished bites is another problem to watch out for. I confess this is a problem area I suffer from myself and often see others fall into this trap. Any boat restoration is full of distractions and tangents to perk interest over the given task at hand. Sometimes this is because another task looks like more fun or you simply see something else not on the list that needs attention. Usually the thought is "Well, I will just fix this over here real quick." The problem is this adds time and effort for something that may not be as important. If you need to switch gears and move onto another task for any reason, be careful to return and finish the one you left as soon as possible. Just another reason for having a good plan and sticking to it.

▲ All they need now is a boat.

Speaking of distractions, do not get carried away with setting up your work area or on elaborate tool setups. I have seen some folks take more than a year just to get their shop and work area set up. Of course you are going to have to spend some time in preparing to work but keep it simple. If you really enjoy the work and plan on restoring boats for some time to come, then a really well set up shop would be an asset. If you are just doing one boat to get yourself out on the water then less effort could be put into the ideal work area. Keep this in mind when purchasing tools as well. If you only need a tool for a single job it would be better to rent or borrow it. The same would apply for a shelter while working on the boat. For a single project a simple cover made of PVC pipe and Visqueen plastic would be suitable. I have seen some restorers spend the better part of their budget on a work shelter that would only be torn down when the project was complete. We all want to sit down to a meal at a fine oak table with polished silverware but sometimes a picnic table and plastic utensils will work.

Don't overlook the small stuff either. Any restoration is made up of a few large tasks and many smaller ones. As mentioned, I often like to leave the little jobs as side or filler work. This works well but do not leave the small stuff for too long or, as the restoration comes to an end, you will find yourself with a bunch of little unfinished tasks. Enjoy the side dishes along with the main course.

Think about how you are going to eat that elephant. Take the time to do the proper planning. Maintain your plan to keep an eye on the overall budget. Try to work efficiently by staying focused and having side tasks to work on when you get held up on the main or larger task. Try to maintain the style and build quality, particularly with things that show. Don't let your work stand out like a sore thumb, have it blend in to look original. Try to remain consistent with the work. Most project boats are formidable meals and you need to keep taking bites to finish them. Don't forget about the side dishes but don't take on too many of them. Stay focused on moving ahead one bite at a time.

6 Finances and Budgeting

Controlling costs and resources is a key part of every project boat and very often the one thing that will make or break a restoration. Although not something most like to think about or even deal with, it is very important and deserves attention.

Budgeting is more than just counting beans and spread sheets; it is a way of planning and hopefully controlling project resources in general. Most think of budgeting in terms of managing money but when it comes to project management, budgeting also includes managing the time or man hours to work on the boat and any other resources that may be limited. As many have learned the hard way, it is far too easy to lose control of spending when working on a boat. It is common to underestimate just how much money will be needed

▲ All it takes is money. *Photo courtesy of Pexels.com.*

for any restoration project. Most people take on a project boat because they think it will be a good way to save money. Although the initial cost may be low, expenses can and do add up quickly. Equipment, storage, relocation, parts, and so on all quickly adds to the cost of your project. It is very important to monitor and control costs from the very beginning.

Personally I am not that big on keeping ledgers and such, but with computers and easy to use accounting software tracking and monitoring your restoration expenses is not all that difficult, it just takes a bit of time and consistency. Although it can be tedious at times, it will be worth the effort. It is important to know where and when your hard-earned cash is going into your project. In order to control expenses and not get in too deep, it helps to know just how your money is being spent and when you will have to spend it in the future. It is amazing just how quickly things can get out of control

▲ This one may not be worth the effort.

and you suddenly find yourself in over your head or worse, in too much debt. This is why it is so important to plan and control expenses throughout the project cycle.

There is often a temptation at the start of a project to not worry about just how much you are spending. You are just getting started and money is not a big concern . . . yet. Let's face it— most people, myself included, do not really bother to keep track of every nickel and dime we are putting into our boats. When we first start on the restoration we are full of enthusiasm and want to go full speed ahead. With everything else we have to think about, money is often not our first concern. However, it is important to understand that when you get a project boat you are opening a hole into another dimension that money will constantly flow into. You can control how fast it flows, but as long as you have the boat it will be like a black hole that wants to suck in all your spare cash.

A key concept which I talked about before is not putting more into your boat than it may be worth when completed. Hopefully you did your homework before purchasing your project and have estimated what it will take to restore the boat as well as what its ultimate resale value will be. As mentioned, it is important not to spend more on the boat than you will be able to sell it for. Once again, I understand the argument that this boat may be for you and you plan to keep it forever, therefore resale value is not important. But keep in mind at some point you might be forced to sell the boat. Also keep in mind that just because you spend $10,000 on the boat, does not mean it will be worth $10,000 more—it just does not work like that. Value is based on overall condition and market conditions for similar boats. This is important to understand not only for resale but for insurance purposes as well. You do not want to have a lot more money into a boat than you can get it insured for. Insurance companies do not care what you have put into it, all they care about is what similar boats are worth.

Not spending more than the boat will sell for is another good reason not to get carried away and start gutting or redesigning

▲ A nicely done restoration.

the boat. It would clearly cost more to do a complete redesign and rebuild when it might not really be needed or add any value. Bringing the boat back to original condition before any modifying or adding new features will save money and help control costs. It also helps to avoid getting in upside down, or dare I say it, "underwater" when it comes to the boat's value. Get the basics done and only then should you start doing rework or modifications to fit your personal needs and likes.

Without trying to sound discouraging, it is a fact that nobody, myself included, ever spends less than they expected on a boat restoration. Now I am sure it has happened and I am also sure unicorns exist, but you get my point. I know everyone thinks it will cost less than it does, and that they will be the ones to be able to pull it off under budget. The fact of the matter is almost everyone underestimates the real costs. This not because they think they can do better or are smarter, it is because it is almost impossible to predict all of the problems that they may encounter. Cost overruns can occur due to things we have no control over such as rising costs of supplies or unscrupulous subcontractors. The only people I have heard of coming out way ahead are the boat flippers who cut corners at every opportunity. These folks are just in it to make a fast buck at the expense of an unaware buyer and often do substandard work.

Years ago, I read one of those self-help get-rich-quick books and although I did not get rich, one concept it talked about made a lot of sense. It was a theory having to do with sustaining a positive attitude through the assumption of a negative result. What the author meant was one should assume the worst and be prepared for the worst case to help stay positive. You will not be disappointed if you expect things to be challenging and they do not work out how you prepared since you planned for the worst. On the other hand, if things go well you can be pleasantly surprised. I have found over the years this applies well to boat restoration. Plan for the worst and be prepared for it. This line of thinking applies well when planning a boat restoration budget. Plan to spend more than you think you will and if you are wrong, you will then have beer and sailing money left over, right? On the other hand, if you underestimate everything you will become frustrated and discouraged when cost overruns happen. So plan for the worst and work towards the best.

One of the better reasons for getting a project boat is that it does allow you to control costs. For many it is not possible to buy a fully found boat without having to finance at least a part of the purchase price. When you owe the bank, they expect you to make the same payment every month. With a project boat you can, for the most part, control how much money you put into the boat each month. If you are having a good month and maybe your great-aunt left you a few extra bucks, you can put more into your restoration. On the other hand, if your car breaks down or your hours at work get cut back, you can reduce your project spending until finances improve. As a self-employed person myself, this has always been an appealing part of doing a project boat. Being able to control how much I spend and when I spend it is easier to deal with than worrying about making a bank payment on time. It also means the boat is owned outright and no money is owed on it.

In the previous chapter, I covered planning the work. Now it is time to plan the money to go with that work. You should have at least a ballpark figure at this point of just what it will cost to complete your restoration. If you have not done so, now is the time to get that pencil and paper out and start playing with the numbers. Be realistic and then double it, you may come close to what you will end up spending. This is where most fail to understand, or perhaps deny the reality of what a boat restoration really costs. It is better

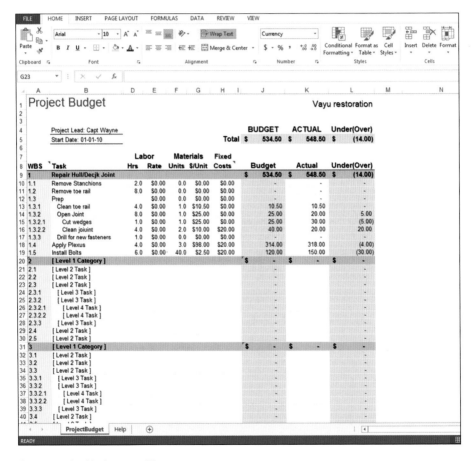

▲ An example of budget spreadsheet.

to overestimate and end up spending less, than to underestimate and not have the resources to complete the restoration. It is not an easy task, even many boatyards struggle with estimates. The more real experience you have working on boats the closer to the actual cost estimates you will be, but remember it is always better to overestimate than to underestimate.

Planning your budget is a lot like planning the work except you work backwards. When planning the tasks you have to start breaking things down and work from the biggest task to the smallest. For example, to restore the boat you have to fix the engine, to fix the engine you have to replace the head gasket, to replace the head gasket you have to take the head off, and so on. When working on a budget the process is reversed. Because you know what each task is you can estimate the cost working from the smaller tasks to the bigger until you have a good idea of the overall cost. In the above example, you add the cost of the head gasket and parts along with the cost of an outside machine shop to the overall project. This can be done with each task you set up when planning the work. You then would add in some amount for miscellaneous small and expendable supplies such as rags, cleaning supplies, gloves, brushes, and so on. When adding it all up, throw in another 10 to 20 percent.

I have always used a simple spreadsheet to set this up. Using a spreadsheet will assist in understanding the full scope of the project and help break it down into manageable bits. The further you break down the tasks into smaller ones, the better your results will be up to a point; you do not want to get so detailed you spend more time on the spreadsheet than working on the boat. Once the tasks are set up it is easy to set up columns for cost estimates along with actual costs and the difference between estimated costs and actual costs. Knowing all these numbers will help keep you on track and give you the information needed to make adjustments to the plans when needed. Many software packages are available to do this and will make all the data entry easier by allowing you to only have to enter the information once.

By creating this work/budget list you can now begin to plan a timeline for how things will proceed. You should estimate how long each task should take, allowing you to plan the sequence of how the work will be done. With this information, it is possible to plan when you will need funds for certain projects and when the best times to do some tasks will be. With any project, the expenses are not going to flow in a steady stream; it will be more like waves and tides. There will be times when not much money needs to be spent, such as when re-varnishing an interior or doing a small woodworking project. At other times a large amount of cash may be needed, for example when rebuilding an engine or doing major electrical work. Having a plan for this will help save for the bigger expenses when they arrive.

Of course, all this needs to match available funds, something that is often a challenge. It may be necessary to adjust plans slightly to meet resources. It is important to be realistic, keeping in mind that cost overruns are to be expected. A bit of a buffer needs to be allowed for in all planning. It may be necessary to do a bit of triage on the task

▲ Avoid the charge. *Photo courtesy of Pexels.com.*

list if the amount of work exceeds the budget. You should determine what really needs to be done as opposed to what you might like to do. For example, replacing the cutlass bearing is more important than installing a new stereo. At some point it may be necessary to focus on the really important tasks and leave the fun projects for later. A good budget will allow you to do this and plan accordingly.

When working out the budget, it is important to have an understanding of credit as well. Credit can be useful but it can also be a trap that can be hard to get out of. It can be very easy to get into trouble with credit card debt when cash flow is slow and you want to keep progress moving. It can be tempting to just charge something when you are in the heat of the battle and funds run low or when you have a larger expense that might require more cash than you have on hand at the moment.

Do not get me wrong, credit cards can be useful and can help keep project momentum moving but you have to be careful not to get in too far over your head. Try to have just one card for use on the boat projects. Set a realistic (and somewhat low) credit limit on this one card. Do not allow the bank to raise that limit without your approval either, as many of them have a tendency to do that. Having a single card will also help with accounting, as you will not be mixing boat and personal expenses. Keep in mind it is important to pay off balances as quickly as possible to avoid interest charges; boats cost enough without having to add additional expenses to the mix. Money spent on interest could be put to better use on the boat. It is hard to completely avoid using credit cards these days but interest can be avoided by picking the right card and paying off balances in a timely fashion each month. You might even be able to get bonus points on your card for purchases that can later be redeemed for more boat parts.

There are times when it might be worth a bit extra spent on interest, though. When searching for used parts you never know when you will come across a good deal on something you may not need at the moment but are sure you will need in the future. Being able to take advantage of such a situation may well be worth a bit more spent on interest but be careful not to trick yourself. It is by far better if a savings account can be set up for those times when a good deal floats by.

An alternative to credit card debt could be a regular bank loan. This is often a good choice when you have a large expense such as a new motor or new sails. Interest is typically lower and you can set a longer term to pay it off. As with credit cards, you should be careful not to take on more than you can pay off quickly. Banks also may ask for collateral and this could be the boat itself. This could be a problem should you run into financial difficulty. That said, banks rarely want to seize a boat, particularly a project boat, so should the worst happen, they would likely want to work with you. Of course it is always better not to have any loans out on the boat at all.

In order to avoid using credit, it helps to have some savings set aside for the restoration. If you know you are going to be getting a project boat it would be a good idea to start a savings account while you are searching for one. Try to put away as much as possible so you will be able to dip into savings instead of pulling out that credit card. Having this buffer can really help and will save with interest expenses and other bank fees. As they say, "cash is king" and when it comes to getting that really good deal on a used part, having some cash on hand to take advantage of it is always a good thing. Even when funds are really tight I try to keep something in savings for the boat at all times.

Budgeting does not always have to do with money matters. As mentioned, there are other resources that require careful budgeting. Time is among the more important of these. However, time is not exactly the same as money in the sense that time is never static. Time marches on and once gone can never be gotten back. Unlike money you cannot save or bank time. You can, however, find ways to use less of it and get more done with the time you do have. On the other hand, time can be like money in that there is never enough of it, it always takes more than you planned, and it is always hard to

▲ Staying on time.

get more of. Time is also like money since it is something you do not want to waste and is another killer of project boats. Things always take longer than expected; keeping this in mind will help you use time wisely.

Time management is as important as money management and should be given the same care when planning. As with money, underestimating the amount of time needed to complete tasks can lead to frustration. Unlike money, you cannot go out and simply earn more of it when needed so time needs to be used carefully. Wasted time cannot be gained back. Be realistic when planning time spent on the boat and leave time for family and friends as well. I try to leave at least one work day a week for boat work. I also look for time that might otherwise be wasted to get in a little extra boat work. I have brought bits of the boat home with me and did painting or varnishing in the evening after dinner. I find this relaxing and a good way to unwind at the end of a long work day. It is a better use of time than zoning out in front of the TV like I usually do after work. Finding little blocks of time like this can help the project along.

Everyone is different and how we best use time depends on your own personality but the important thing is to try to be consistent and maintain momentum with the work. For some this may be setting up specific times to do boat work while others may like to remain a bit more casual and flexible. The important thing is to have a set number of hours to get boat work done each week. You do not want to be so rigid that the work is no longer fun but some self-discipline is required if the restoration is to be completed in a timely fashion. It can be far too easy to put things off and find yourself on a seemingly endless project. Building a time budget and trying to stick to it will help. The trap many fall into is slowly letting the time spent on the boat trickle off until one day they are simply no longer doing any real work and the

▲ Using professional help.

project languishes. This can be a real problem when work has to stop for a while due to any number of outside influences such as health, job, or family.

Time management also needs to take into account weather, the seasons, and other outside influences. This is another good reason to have several tasks going at the same time. For rain days or other bad weather days it helps to have a task or two set aside to work on inside. This way progress continues even though it may not be just what you had planned for that day. Having a few tasks that are not time-critical you can stop and start will help keep the workflow moving forward. It is also important when planning larger projects to take the season into account. Winter cold and summer heat can make it difficult or impossible to get some tasks done. All this needs to be considered when setting up a time budget.

When planning for time it is also important to consider those times when you may need outside help with a task. It is easy to be flexible with your own time but if requesting help, you do not want to waste others' time. Friends or even paid subcontractors will need some advance planning. Plan for this carefully so you will know in

▲ Sunset awaits.

advance when you need this type of help. This will allow you to have everything ready when your help shows up as scheduled.

When planning time, I like to use the old tortoise and hare theory. Slow and steady is better than everything at once. This tends to be another classic mistake many make. When they first get their project boat they jump in with both feet and put in a lot of time and effort. It can be hard to maintain this intense workflow and things soon begin to slow down. It is best to proceed at a nice, even pace as this will be easier to maintain over the long term. It is often a long race so pacing yourself is important.

As mentioned, remember to keep some time for yourself and your family as well. You do not want those close to you to become resentful of the time spent on the boat and you do not want to work so hard you get burned out before the project is complete. Many project boats take months and sometimes years to complete. It is important to leave time for other things that you enjoy as well as to spend time with those close to you. Working on the boat can be a great escape from the daily grind but it should not become an excuse to avoid family. It has been shown that efficiency actually improves when regular breaks are taken so add these in your time budget from the start.

Whether you are budgeting time, money, or supplies it is important to remain flexible and always be adjusting and updating the budget. Project boats are full of surprises and some tasks will take longer than expected while others may take less. Adjustments will need to be made to reflect changes as the work progresses. It is important not to just set up a budget and leave it static, it will need constant adjusting and tweaking as the project proceeds. By adjusting the budget you may find some tasks will have to be put off while others moved up on the priority list. This is why it is important to adjust as the work proceeds.

Although budgeting is just another task to do with a project boat and may not seem that important, it does help in planning work and finances and helps find and track problem areas. It does not take an accountant to do this. Even a very simple budget is better than no budget. It may not be the most exciting part of the work but it will help ensure the restoration goes smoother and will save money in the end.

7 Bits and Pieces

Every boat is made up of many pieces. Some big, some small, but they all add up to a finished boat ready to head to sea. It is crucial to any boat restoration to get the right parts at the right price at the right time to keep the work moving forward. Sourcing the parts needed is a critical part of any restoration project. It might not be as easy as it sounds. Finding parts that are no longer made for an older or classic boat can be a challenge. Even standard parts require careful sourcing to save money and time. Knowing where to find parts and where to get good deals on them is an important part of any successful project. If not sourced carefully, the cost of parts alone could exceed the value of the boat.

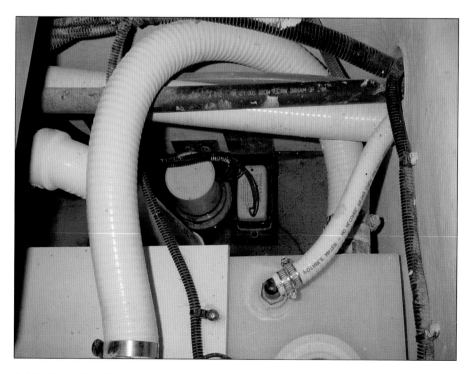

▲ Lots of parts down there.

Purchasing parts when needed and at the best possible price is critical to keeping the budget under control. This is an area where would-be restorers sometimes make several major mistakes that can unfortunately doom the project early on. One of the first mistakes they make is buying the wrong parts at the wrong time—parts they really don't need or won't use until much later in the project. When taking on a restoration, the rule of thumb is to only buy what you need when you need it. I am often a bit mystified when I see someone purchase items that will not be needed until the restoration is almost complete. Electronics, safety gear, and other items not required right away should not be purchased until the project is close to completion even if those items appear to be a really good deal at the time.

The only reason to buy any parts before they are needed is if you are getting a killer deal that you know may never come around again. Even then there are some things that can wait to be purchased. Safety equipment and electronics top this list. In the fast-paced electronics market it does not take long for today's latest and greatest to become tomorrow's obsolete technology. What may seem like a good deal now may not be useful by the time it is needed. Safety equipment often has a limited lifespan as well. Flares, fire extinguishers, and life rafts all have expiration or recertification dates and require replacement or regular inspections. There is little point in obtaining this type of equipment until you are at the end of the restoration. Before purchasing anything, ask yourself if this is something that is needed right away, and if not, is the deal really so good that it should be bought anyway?

This is another reason for setting up a plan and budget as this will guide you in knowing just what parts and supplies are needed and when they are needed. There are exceptions such as hard to find parts that when located should be purchased but for the most part it is a good idea to only get what you need when it is needed. This is a pretty basic concept in business these days with factories only having parts delivered to the assembly line literally minutes before needed.

▲ At the parts store.

This not only saves storage space but does not tie up money in parts that may just be sitting around unused for months and sometimes years. Another reason for not getting too many parts ahead of time is storage. Any parts that are not immediately needed will need to be stored and protected from damage. This is another burden on the project as a whole. Unused parts can also clutter up the work and storage areas, making it hard to find what you really need.

Sourcing parts and supplies and getting the best deals on those parts and supplies is a big part of any project and requires a fair amount of time to do correctly. It would be easy if everything needed could just be picked up at the local marine supply store but as we all know nothing is ever that easy when it comes to boats. Many parts for older boats may not be available while others may not be cost-effective to buy new. The trick is finding the right parts at the right price. There are many sources for parts and supplies, some better than others. Thanks to the Internet getting what you need is easier than it ever has been. With online outlets it is now possible to literally search the whole world for just that right part. You can even check local sources online before setting off to the store. This can be a mixed blessing in that it takes a bit of knowhow not to get lost in this vast world of cyber shopping.

No matter the size of your restoration, the first source of parts and supplies will usually be local outlets. This would include local marine supply retailers along with hardware stores, big box home improvement stores, and local wholesalers. These are the go-to places for all the smaller bits and pieces needed along with the sundry supplies such as nuts, bolts, screws, painting supplies, and the like. Usually the best source of local marine parts and supplies are wholesalers that sell to local marinas, repair yards, and local subcontractors. These wholesalers will usually have a good selection

▲ The marine section in a hardware store.

as well as the best prices. I try to avoid the major marine chain stores that often do not discount much from list prices. Sadly, many of the smaller mom and pop retail outlets have gone under and have been replaced with the larger chain stores so in many locations your choices may be limited. The chain stores can be good if you just have to have something now but you will have to pay more for that convenience.

Marine wholesalers tend to offer a broader selection of basic repair supplies and tools along with other hardware and equipment. This is because they cater to the boatyards and repairers that use a lot of these materials. But not all wholesale outlets are willing to work with a single individual just working on their own boat. Most do not have a storefront and will only deliver to your location. They rarely want to add another stop to their route, particularly if you are not purchasing thousands of dollars' worth of supplies from them. Most wholesalers will likely require you have a state tax ID number as they do not collect sales taxes, meaning you will have to pay those directly to the state. All this makes it a bit harder to get an account as an individual. But do not be discouraged—it is worth talking to these folks and letting them know you have a restoration going. Depending on the size and scope of the project, they may be willing to work with you.

If the project you are working is large enough, you may consider starting a small company to operate under for the restoration. By operating under a business name you will be in a better position to buy from wholesalers and other suppliers at a discount. Starting a small business will allow legitimacy when it comes to negotiating with suppliers but it does mean more recordkeeping and you will be responsible for paying your own state sales and use taxes. Working under the umbrella of a business may also have some advantages with insurance and liability. If considering this option, you should talk to an attorney to find out if it's worthwhile. Keep in mind a business does have additional costs and recordkeeping rules adding to the project overhead.

▲ Nice to have to have them together.

Another option for working with wholesalers is to buy through an independent subcontractor. These small, often one-man operations will likely have accounts already set up with most of the local suppliers. They may be willing to allow you to purchase through them. They can make a bit by having a small markup while you still save. In many cases the amount of discount a company or subcontractor gets is based on how much they purchase every year. For a small, one-man business, having you purchase through them will increase their annual sales, giving them a better discount. This could benefit both of you in the long run. Of course this requires getting to know some of the local subcontractors, and if you can use their services from time to time as well it will help develop a good working relationship.

Other sources for local parts and supplies are hardware and automotive stores. I do caution, however, about using non-marine grade supplies. There are some cases where you may be able to save a few bucks by buying non-marine but having been in this business for many years, I can assure you marine grade is, most of the time, better. Silicone sealant is a classic example of this. The quality of silicone for home and bath is not suitable for marine use. You can get better grade building quality silicone but it will cost the same as the marine grade. Basically you get what you pay for. Be careful when purchasing stainless steel supplies such as screws, nuts, and bolts as not all stainless is the same quality. Always take the time to know just what you are buying or the savings may end up costing more in the long run. That said, it can be helpful to buy certain items from non-marine sources. Hardware stores and big box home improvement stores are often a good source for lumber, plumbing fittings, and basic supplies such as sandpaper, solvents, and masking tape.

▲ Shopping for supplies.

There are times when a part may be needed right away and the only option is the name brand marine chain stores. There are ways to save from these outlets as well. Talk to the manager and let them know you are working on a restoration project. Many have discounts for commercial customers and may extend the same discounts to those with bigger projects. These discounts can vary and may not be as much as one would hope for but every little bit helps. Once again, you may need a tax number to open a commercial account but check with them and see what they can do for you.

If you are working out of a boatyard with a ships store, they are often a good source for parts that are needed right away. Like the chain stores they may not be the cheapest source of parts, but the convenience may well be worth the higher price. Some boatyards may give a discount if you let them know you are going to be buying more than the average boat owner. If you are hiring the yard to help with some work this may also be in your favor for getting better prices. Try to get to know and befriend some of the yard management, buy the crew doughnuts, and in general try to be a good customer. This good will can pay off in discounts and other help when you need it.

With proper planning, ordering parts and supplies online can provide substantial savings over the brick and mortar local sources. Online retailers offer not only better prices but very often a better selection. Keep in mind that not all online retailers are the same and some are better than others. A bit of research and checking online feedback will help when selecting an online vendor. Do not just shop price alone. Always check shipping costs and any handling or hidden fees before clicking that "Place Order" button. Any company that adds handling charges or other fees should be avoided. Many companies will offer free shipping with a minimum order so it may pay to order enough supplies to meet this minimum. Another way to save with larger companies is to check for discount codes to be used when placing orders. These can sometimes be as much as 20 percent so it is worth checking into. Companies often email these discounts to existing customers. If you are not an existing customer, they can sometimes be found by searching online.

▲ A selection of parts.

Beyond the traditional online stores are auction and reseller sites such as eBay and Amazon. These sources both offer new and used parts and supplies although Amazon tends to focus on new while eBay focuses on used items. Both these sites are a good location for startup businesses into the marine retail market to offer their goods. This can sometimes be a good thing as they are very price competitive. On the other hand, many newer companies do not have a track record to verify them as good sellers. For this reason, eBay and Amazon offer some buyer protections should you have a problem with a seller. Be sure to read over and understand these protection plans before ordering. They both allow several vendors to be searched in one location which can save time shopping when you know what you need. This helps with price comparison when shopping for new and used parts. Along with startups, I have found that many well-known and established companies may use Amazon or eBay to sell off closeout items at a discount. Established companies sell through these sources so as not to compete against themselves on their own websites.

Always check return policies when ordering online as these can vary and can be important in case you get the wrong part. Return policies can really make a big difference with who you buy from so it pays to read the fine print. It may be worth spending a bit more from a seller that has a good record of handling returns. Some sellers will pay return shipping but most do not anymore. Many have a set time period for making returns such as ten days from receipt. If that time is less than ten days I would pass them up. Thirty days is a better period to allow time for checking parts. On the subject of time limits, make sure the seller has a good record of prompt refunds back to your credit card. Some sellers will only issue a store credit for a refund which is not really the same thing as a cash refund. Mistakes happen, sometimes it is from using the wrong part number or the seller will ship the wrong item. Being able to make an easy return and get a prompt refund is important. It helps to read online reviews for a seller paying attention to customer feedback.

Of course you do not always have to buy new. There are many sources for used parts as well. Used parts are not only less expensive, but in the case of classic boats they may be the only way to find matching or original parts. As with new parts, there are several outlets to find used parts. Most towns located near larger boating centers will likely have used and surplus ships stores. Many of these stores sell both retail and used parts. Some will sell on consignment while others purchase used gear and resell it. In most cases, prices can be negotiated to some degree. It often pays to barter a bit when shopping these outlets as the listed price is usually a starting point. Often the owners of these used outlets will help you locate a specific part if you let them know what you are looking for. This can help broaden your search when looking for those hard to find items. Used part stores are fun to poke around in; you never know just what you will find. As mentioned earlier though, resist the temptation to open your wallet unless you find something you really need.

Working boatyards will sometimes sell used parts but you will have to ask as they do not always display used parts in their stores. It never hurts to ask if there is something you are looking for. I find the higher end yards that do major refits will often have the best used gear. Some yards will hold an annual yard sale, or flea market, where they sell some of their used gear and invite customers to sell gear as well. These used gear sales can be fun to poke around at and you never know when you might find a good deal on a needed item. It can take a bit of homework to find when and where these flea markets are. Stop by to visit some local boatyards and ask to be put on their mailing list if they have these sales. This way you will know when these sales are being held.

Although they are becoming a bit scarcer in this digital age, local classified flyers that list used cars and boats will often have a used parts section. Back in my day we had the *Pennysaver* and other

▲ Shopping the flyers.

tabloid weekly classifieds that would list used cars, boats, and boat parts along with other merchandise. These were a good source for local used parts particularly larger items that might be costly to ship. In today's cyber world these print classifieds have mostly been replaced with online listings, the same concept just online instead of in print. Craigslist is the best known of these but there may be others in your local area. Unlike eBay and Amazon, there is no buyer protection when dealing directly with the seller through these sources. If meeting a seller in person, always be sure to meet in a public location. Make sure you know what you are getting and if possible get a receipt with the seller's phone number and address. Never meet someone alone and always let others know when and where you are meeting someone. Problems are rare but it never hurts to be cautious.

There may other sources for local parts such as local boating and yacht clubs. They may have annual flea markets or classified listings in their newsletters as well. Do a bit of hunting and asking around

▲ Shopping on eBay.

and I am sure you will find other sources like these. If looking for hard to find parts it helps to put the word out wherever you can. Consider making business cards with your contact info and maybe a tag line stating you are looking for boat parts.

I have found eBay to be one of the best sources for used boat parts. My experience has been most sellers are just boaters looking to sell parts they do not need so they can buy parts they do need. Not everyone feels comfortable buying from strangers online and I understand that. However, with the protections eBay and PayPal provide, purchasing online has become much safer. Most sellers allow returns and even those that do not will have to take a part back if it is not as stated in the listing. The trick to finding hard to get parts and getting a good price is to take your time. It is worth the time and effort to set up some watch lists and check them often. This will help find the hard to get parts as well as help spot a good deal when it comes along. If you expect to get online and find a part right away you may be disappointed or end up paying too much. I have spent a year or more looking for the right part at the right price—once again a good reason for proper planning. If you know what you are going to need in advance you can take your time to find exactly that needed part at a good price.

There are a few things you can do to ensure buying used parts online through eBay is a painless experience. When looking at listings, make sure there is a photo of the actual part being sold, not a stock photo or a photo of a similar part. Check the seller's feedback rating; if they have a lot of recent negative feedback you might want to look elsewhere. Pay attention to shipping costs; I have seen sellers listing items at a very low sale price only to have outrageously high shipping costs. I generally avoid buying from foreign sellers as this tends to complicate things and not all of them are legitimate. Be careful of second chance offers or the seller contacting you directly to buy or pay for anything outside of the eBay envelope. If you happen to run into problems, try to contact the seller prior to filing a complaint but keep all contact within the eBay email system and always be cordial and polite. If a complaint needs to be filed, your previous communications will be reviewed by eBay staff. If you do need to return anything, always require a signature from the person receiving the package. This may be your only proof it was returned and you will not receive a refund without this.

There are some supplies that are best bought in bulk. These include lumber, glues, fasteners, and the like. When planning it can be hard to know every screw and bolt that may be needed so it is good to keep a stock of these things. I like to set up a small parts "room" or a few shelves where I keep the supplies organized and easy to find. Supplies like lumber and fasteners are always good to have on hand and they can be stored for as long as needed. Other supplies such as paints, glues, and resins tend to have a limited shelf live so you want to make sure you only have just as much as you need on hand. This can be particularly true with some of the newer adhesives, paints,

▲ Marine supplies.

and sealants. Care also needs to be used when storing these items with regard to temperature and humidity.

Just what supplies will be needed depends on your particular project and what type of work will be done. For painting and finishing work you will want solvents, sandpaper, masking tape, and the like.

Carpentry projects will require lumber, fasteners, glues, and the like. For electrical work, a good supply of wire, crimp connectors, wires, ties, and other basic electrical parts will be needed. Whatever supplies you may be stocking, keep in mind their shelf life. For items with a limited shelf life check the dates when purchasing and make sure you get the newest stock. Often, this will be the cans in the back of the shelf, sort of like shopping for fresh fruit at the grocery store.

For some restoration projects you will need to get replacement parts to match the original construction. This can be challenging and is not always possible. If your goal is to restore a classic boat such as an old Chris-Craft, there are sites that specialize in stocking original or aftermarket parts to keep the boat as close to original as possible. Items such as original engine gauges and emblems can be found with a little persistence. Online owner's forums specializing in boat restoration can be helpful in locating these hard to find items. You can post what you are looking for and hopefully find someone who either has the needed part or can guide you in the right direction to find it. Sometimes it is possible to find substitute parts for some items that will work while remaining close to original.

Some parts may have to be fabricated; items such as rails, chain plates, and propeller shafts can be fabricated at most local machine shops. Other items such as cast parts might be a bit harder to remake; in these cases a substitution may have to be found. Engine manifolds, water pumps, and other parts may be very difficult to source for older motors. For these parts it pays to start looking early and keep checking every source available. This is where doing your homework becomes important.

For older wooden boats or boats with wood interiors there is the problem of matching woods and wood species. This becomes harder

▲ Lots of wood and varnish here.

as time goes on as old-growth as well as some exotic woods are no longer available. Even the same species of wood may look a lot different or is not the same quality. As the old growth forests disappear, plantation-grown wood may be the only source for many types of lumber. Plantation-grown trees often do not have the same color or grain as the old growth lumber did. These new-growth woods often do not have the same strength characteristics as old-growth lumber did either. In some cases when the same type of wood is available its cost may be very high. Teak is the most common example of this. Back in the 1970s and 1980s, teak was common and relatively cheap. Today, with restrictions on export due to a dwindling supply, good teak is hard to find and very expensive.

There are times when wood substitutions can be made without compromising the look or strength. There are a couple of woods that make a good replacement for teak and are a close match in color and grain. Ipe is less expensive and has many of the same properties as teak; it is a bit darker and heavier but a lot less expensive. Cumaru and Iroko also make good substitutes. Mahogany comes in many varieties that vary in color and grain, so it can be hard to find an exact match unless you can bring a sample to an expert. Most American lumber such as oak and fir are still available but you have to shop the quality as it can vary wildly. To get really good quality lumber you may have to order from a specialty lumber company rather than a local supplier. This requires buying the lumber sight unseen but you can always request that they ship a small piece to check for compatibility before placing a larger order. Most suppliers will not have a problem with this although they will likely charge a small fee for this service.

Boat interiors are often done with veneers. A veneer is a thin layer of wood over plywood to make it look like a solid piece of lumber.

▲ A selection of wood stains.

Veneered plywood often comes in 4 x 8 panels. These larger panels can be expensive to ship so if you only need a small amount, it may be cost-effective to purchase native plywood sheets locally and apply your own veneer as needed. If you do, be sure to use high-quality plywood for the base. You can also achieve the color match needed with stains and tints. It can be a bit tricky to get a good color match, but with a bit of experimenting on scrap wood you can often get good results.

With a good project plan in hand you can get the parts and supplies you need at prices that will not bust your budget. Take the time to shop carefully and do not buy things not needed ahead of time unless the cost savings make it worth your while to store those parts. Avoid buying parts and gear not absolutely needed for the restoration. You can always get the fun stuff after the project is complete. Take the time not spent working on the boat to do a bit of shopping to find what you need. Shop around different sources comparing costs. Sourcing parts can be a bit of a scavenger hunt and it can be fun and exciting when you are able to score that elusive item at a great price.

8 Staying Motivated

Completing a project boat can be a bit like climbing Mount Everest—it is a hard journey and it takes a great deal of persistence and self-motivation to get to the end goal. Granted, you will not have to deal with lack of oxygen and avalanches but a larger project boat can, indeed, make you feel like you are climbing a mountain. If you encounter a couple of major setbacks, it becomes easy to get discouraged and make you feel like giving up. But there is indeed a summit to be achieved and the feeling of accomplishment at having reached the top can make all the effort and hard work worthwhile. The trick is staying motivated until the end. More

▲ An intimidating project.

boat restorations are started than are ever finished. Many of these unfinished boats are a result of their owners running out of motivation before they reached the top.

In the first chapter, I talked about the motivations many have for starting a boat restoration. At the start of any project motivation is the easy part, maintaining that enthusiasm throughout the project is not so easy. Things take longer than expected, costs rise, and problems are encountered. The honeymoon does not always last when the work gets dirty and is no longer as much fun. Problems are encountered and the work begins to drag, taking longer than expected. This is particularly true with larger restoration projects. The work can be dirty, smelly, itchy, and is often done in unpleasant conditions. I often thought Mike Rowe should have done an episode or two of *Dirty Jobs* in a boatyard.

Time after time, I see project boats that are left half-finished. I feel bad for the owners that have put so much effort into something only to slowly give up halfway through. For many, it is because they took on too large a restoration, while for others life sometimes just gets in the way. Jobs change, marriages fail, and health issues can all stop a project dead in its tracks. But for many others, the problem is a simple lack of motivation to keep the project moving. It can be very hard to keep the enthusiasm going when the work drags on, the cost keeps rising, and the work is harder than expected. Slowly, the time spent on the boat decreases; after all there are more fun things to do. Games to watch, time spent with family, and work around the house all compete for time with the boat.

The real trick to completing any boat restoration is staying motivated long enough to see it through to the end. In an effort to stay motivated there are a few tricks to keep in mind. There is a ton of motivational information out there and most of it is useful. I confess though, I am not one to stand in front of a mirror and tell myself how good I will do that day. Maintaining motivation is a bit harder than just doing that. However, there are some other tricks you can use to help maintain motivation. I know everyone is different and what

▲ An unfinished project.

works for one person may not work for another, so the trick is finding what works best for you.

One of the key concepts I have found that works well for me when working on boats (and many things in life for that matter) is something I came across in one of those self-help books so popular in the eighties. I mentioned this earlier but I feel it bears repeating. Years ago, I read a book titled *Winning Through Intimidation* by Robert J. Ringer. Aside from the title, the book had a few great points, one of which I felt made a lot of sense to me and applied well to working on boats: "The Theory of Sustaining a Positive Attitude through the Assumption of a Negative Result." Just what does that mean and how does it apply to boat restoration and staying motivated?

According to this theory, if you want to stay positive and avoid disappointment then assume things are not going to go your way and be prepared for that. Should things work out, you will be happy because you were expecting the worst. If things do go south, then you were prepared for that to happen so it wasn't a surprise or disappointment. I think a simple analogy would be removing a rusty nut from a bolt. Assume the nut will be difficult to come off from the beginning. Be prepared with all the tools needed to remove a thoroughly stuck nut. If the nut comes off easily on the first try you can pack all those tools away and be happy because you were sure it was not coming off. On the other hand, if the nut is truly stuck or worse yet, the bolt breaks, you won't be as frustrated. After all, you had a feeling that was going to happen and at least you were prepared for it. By assuming the worst case it becomes easier to stay positive in the long run. Of course this can be a double-edged sword and staying too negative can just lead to avoiding doing anything for fear it will be too hard. The trick is to stay focused on the positive side of this and realize most things are not as hard as they could be but be prepared just in case. Being prepared will mean less disappointment in the long run and help keep a positive attitude throughout the project.

I have found setting goals and rewards can be another good motivator. With a good project plan in place, it becomes easier to set some basic goals to work towards. I like to divide the bigger goals or tasks into what I call mini goals. I will sometimes break the mini goals down even further into micro goals. If I am really having trouble getting motivated I break the goals down to the point where my micro goal is as simple as getting up and going to get the tools out. I often find that once I have gotten the tools out I might as well go on to the next micro goal and so on until I find I just got closer to or finished the main or mini goal I was working towards. Goals help maintain focus on just one thing at a time as well. Like many, I sometimes have a habit of drifting off the task at hand. Keeping a goal of finishing something with a reward helps direct me back when I find myself wandering. It is harder to talk yourself out of things when you have a simple focus. I have sat in the middle of a project boat and just stared for thirty minutes or more thinking about all the

▲ My kind of reward.

things I have to do. I sometimes feel a bit overwhelmed by it all but when I start breaking each task down in my mind into smaller and smaller chunks, things do not seem as intimidating. The goals, mini goals, and micro goals are really just steps in the overall project plan.

Rewards given to yourself for completing a goal could be simple, such as allowing yourself to take some time off to relax and watch a movie or maybe a nice dinner out. The bigger the goal accomplished, the better the reward should be. It's the proverbial carrot on the stick but it does work. Rewards can also be directed to the project. I like to reward myself by getting a piece of gear that would not normally be part of the standard project but something I would nonetheless like to have. Maybe some new stereo speakers or a shiny new brass clock would be a nice reward. This makes me feel better while helping the overall project at the same time. Whatever works for you is what you should do, the point being to have that carrot out there giving incentive to move forward and get things done.

Of course, no goal is helpful if it is not realistic and trying to get too much done in too short a time or setting a goal that is too hard to complete will likely just lead to frustration and disappointment. By using mini goals, it is possible to take smaller steps and keep the larger goals easily obtainable. People tend to get more satisfaction when they feel they have achieved something, no matter how small. Each mini goal becomes a small victory in itself, helping keep enthusiasm up. However, do not get too caught up in the mini goals and forget that they are there to lead to a larger goal. Big or small, staying focused on the big goal is the objective. Don't get lost in the trees when the forest is the goal.

Focus is another area that tends to get some folks into trouble on a project boat. This is yet another reason for having a project plan and sticking to it! I have seen more than one project boat filled with half-finished jobs. I must confess that has happened to me as well. It is all too easy to get into a particular job only to have to stop for a bit. Parts may run out, glue or paint may need to dry, or for any number of other reasons it may not be possible to proceed. This in turn leads to starting other job before finishing the first. The trick is not to lose focus and forget to return to the unfinished job. Plans and goals can help keep the focus but only if they are followed. This is another reason to reward yourself, but only for finished tasks, not those almost finished.

Along with keeping focused, maintaining momentum is important as well. Basic physics state that it takes more force or energy to get an object moving than it does to keep it moving. This is true with boat restoration as well. It is always harder to pick back up from a hiatus than it is to keep things moving. When working on a boat restoration I try to do a little bit of work almost every day if possible. This does not always mean being on the boat with tools in hand. Very often, it may consist of being at the computer planning or going online and ordering parts. The point is to keep some aspect of the project moving forward. Once work stops for any period of time, it is much harder to start back up again. Parts and pieces seem to just disappear and it is often difficult remembering just what the last thing you were doing was and returning to it. By keeping even a small amount of work going as continuously as possible, it will help keep focus on the project and its completion.

Of course there will be times when the work has to stop for a period as health, family, or even vacations will cause you to set aside boat work for a while. The trick is not to let these breaks become too long or too frequent; otherwise you may find the project has completely stopped. For some it starts slowly, first a short break, then another, and another. Then they find excuses not to do any boat work when the time is available. Each break seems to get a bit longer before getting back to work again. Finally, one day the work stops, never to be restarted. Be aware of this trap and keep the workflow moving, even if slowly. If money is an issue, do things that do not cost much until the cash begins to flow again; if health is an issue, do some planning or paperwork. The trick is to not let the momentum come to a complete stop for anything more than a short period of time.

If, for some reason, the work does need to stop for a while try to leave things at a point where they will be easy to pick back up again. Clean up the work area and leave the boat neat and orderly. Try to have some parts and materials in place so that it will be easy to get right back to work. Do not leave any unfinished tasks if possible, so that when you return to work you can start on fresh projects. Make sure everything is secured to prevent weather damage while you are away. You do not want to get back to work and find damage due to rain or weather just because you did not close it up well enough, Do whatever it takes to make the work easy when you return so you will have fewer excuses not to get back to work.

Momentum does require some persistence to maintain. Persistence is that stubborn determination to keep moving ahead no matter what. Think of it as the mountain climber pushing ahead even when the going is brutal and they are tired and want to give up. Nobody ever

▲ It's not all glamorous.

made it to that summit without a lot of persistence. I have seen many give up when the end was in sight, others may lose motivation early on. Any project is going to have its share of frustrations and setbacks. To make it to the summit takes a certain amount of persistence and determination. Many give up when the work is no longer fun or they find things are taking longer or costing more than they expected. This is when you need persistence more than ever to keep pushing ahead.

Persistence takes a bit more than just wanting something; it takes having the right attitude and displaying self-control. A good attitude can make or break any project but is not always easy to maintain. A good attitude takes constant adjusting and reminding. It is sort of like a car driving down a long straight road. You cannot just set it to go straight and forget about it; you have to keep adjusting the wheel as you go. Attitude is a bit like this as well. It comes naturally to some, but for most of us it takes a bit of work. Let's face it, it is hard to have a good attitude when you are working on that thirty-year-old head system or bundled up in a Tyvek suit grinding fiberglass when it is 96° out on a hot summer afternoon.

It can sometimes be hard to maintain persistence when the work drags. Tasks that end up being harder or taking longer than expected can get you down. This is when you have to kick in the inner mountain climber and slog ahead. There are going to be times when the work is not fun and it seems like it is taking forever to make progress. This is the time to remain persistent and keep the work going. Take a short break for a weekend off to recoup if need be, but once recharged, get back to work. Take a proverbial deep breath before heading up that next hill. This will help keep you moving forward. Make sure you don't allow your quick break to turn into a long vacation or it will be harder to get going again.

When I am feeling particularly frustrated and find myself just not into the work in front of me, I will sometimes shift to a project that might be a bit more fun or more rewarding. Sometimes some paint and varnish work can be a bit Zen-like. A somewhat mindless and relaxing task can help. There is something to be said for doing some rewarding work like varnishing or woodwork that offers a bit of instant gratification along with being relatively easy to do. Whatever type of work is most fun for you would be a good break from fighting that head system or other tedious tasks. Doing something that is a bit showy can be good as well so that you can see the fruits of your labor. I enjoy the reward of being able to admire a new paint job or nicely waxed hull. It helps me feel that I have accomplished something. Pulling wire may be just as important but does not offer the same satisfaction to help with motivation. Doing something that you can sit back and admire thinking *Yeah, that really looks better* is always a nice treat.

There will be times when some good old-fashioned self-discipline is needed. Sometimes I have to force myself to get the gears turning and do some work. It is not always easy but I have found that I almost always feel better after having forced myself to do some work. It can

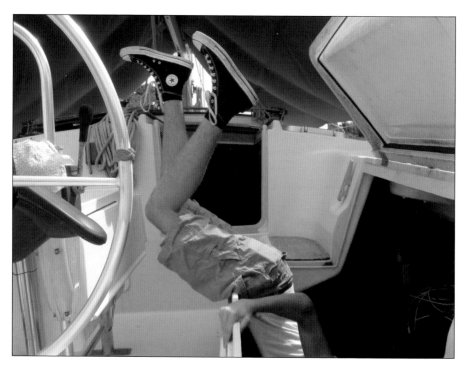

▲ Sometimes it isn't easy.

be hard to be motivated when I am tired and would rather watch a little TV. A bit of self-discipline goes a long way to keeping the work moving ahead. Lack of self-discipline is something that causes many to ultimately fail. For some, self-discipline comes naturally but for most of us it does take a bit of effort.

Yes, there will be times when the work is not fun, you will be tired, and it will be hard. If you do not want your project boat to end up like so many others out there, you have to have the persistence of that mountain climber. You have to be willing to keep going when you really just want to stay at home and watch the game with a cold beer. Years ago, I studied Taekwondo and made it to the rank of second degree black belt. It was not easy and there were many days I got off work and simply did not want to go to the dojo to work out. But every time I forced myself to go, I came home feeling better not only for the workout but for having had the persistence to keep training and making progress towards my goals. So push ahead and get the work done even if you are not in the mood or are tired. In the end you will feel better about the project and yourself as well.

Finishing smaller projects can also be very motivating. Checking jobs off the "to do" list is very motivating even if they are small ones. It is always easier to start a task than to finish one. Some folks are great at starting jobs but not so great at finishing them. This is why it important to actually complete things if the overall project is to be fully completed. There are several reasons a task might get held up other than just losing focus. A lack of parts or supplies among other things can cause a task to be put on hold but it is important to circle back as soon as possible to complete the task. It will also give you a feeling of accomplishment as well as reducing the work list. I see it as having small victories to add encouragement to finish the whole project. After all, no war was ever won if small battles weren't won along the way. Each battle is a step to the winning the war. Each completed task will give encouragement to move on to the next one and give hope that there is an end in sight. Being surrounded by incomplete jobs will just lead to discouragement and frustration, so finish the small jobs as soon as you can. I like to cross completed tasks off my list by putting a line through them but leaving them on the list. This way I get to look back and see all I have accomplished. Even when doing lists on the computer I do not delete completed items; I "line" them out so I can see just how much I have done.

I have found that keeping the boat and work area clean will also help boost motivation. Cleaning up the work area has some obvious benefits, including making it easier and safer to work on as well as being able to find tools and parts without having to dig through a mess. It also has the benefit of subtly improving attitude and helping improve overall positive feeling about the project as a whole. As they say, clutter in the work area leads to clutter in the mind, resulting in a less positive feeling. Putting away unused tools, parts, and supplies will not only make the work area safer, it will improve how you feel about the project as a whole. Clearing the deck, so to speak, allows

▲ Keeping the work area tidy.

you to focus on the job at hand without a lot of little things getting in your way or distracting you. I find it helps to fully clean the boat inside and out from time to time, particularly on a larger long-term project. I see many project boats that just look dirty, mildewed, and in general, not very shipshape. I have found I always feel a bit more positive about things when I take a break and clean things up a bit and maybe even wax the exterior. A nice, clean and shiny boat helps improve the spirit along with motivation.

Another reason to have your project cleaned up and orderly is to keep the boat usable if at all possible. Keeping the boat usable and getting to take it out occasionally is a great way to inspire and motivate. Being able to use the boat every now and then will be a good reminder as to why you are doing all the work you are. It will also help with the feeling that there is indeed light at the end of the tunnel. I have taken many trips with my current project boat although I would not consider it finished by any means. However, I did finish all the mechanical and electrical work first, so I can use the boat while finishing up all the cosmetic stuff. For most of us, being able to use the boat is why we took on the project in the first place so being able to get out on the water can really help with attitude and motivation. Keep in mind, though, that the boat should only be taken out if it can be done safely. Make sure all the proper safety equipment is aboard as well.

For some, fear can slow things down and kill motivation. Fear can stop us dead in our tracks and it comes in many forms. For some it might be the fear of tackling a job they have never done before, the fear of the unknown. Others can be afraid the work will take too long to complete. I often find myself putting things off, thinking I will not finish a task in the time I have available, a fear in its own right. Fear comes in many forms and may not be as obvious as we think yet it can nonetheless stop us from getting things done. The tricky part is we may not always recognize fear as it can be subtle. If you find yourself making excuses for not doing a task you might want to think about if it has anything to do with an underlying fear. Fear is pretty easy to deal with once it is recognized. You just have to acknowledge the fear and understand that it may not be as bad as you think. You have to be willing to look it square in the eye and say "Screw you, I am getting this done!" Fear, as with other problems, can be worked around.

If you're a Star Wars fan, you may recall in Episode VI the speeder chase in the forest. The heroes were zipping around the forest at high speed to avoid the bad guys. They had to constantly dodge around the trees in their path and of course when the bad guys did not they crashed into a tree in a ball of flames. So what does this have to do with motivation and boat restoration? Well anytime you are working on a boat there are a lot of trees in your path. Broken bolts, hidden dry rot, unseen electrical issues, money problems, not having the right tool, the list goes on. All these things are like trees in your path and you have to learn to just zip around them to avoid crashing and burning. A lot of people try to plow through these opportunities when they crop up but this is a mistake. It is always easier to find the path of least resistance and just go around problems as best you can. Of course some problems will have to be dealt with eventually, but I try not to let them bring me to a standstill. For example, if I am working on something and find that I need a part or tool I do not have, I will not stop work and run out to get that missing item. I either work around it or move on to something else in the meantime. By continuing to work, I don't waste any time and reduce my frustration. This is another reason to have a few jobs in progress at any given time. It allows you to move around a bit to keep the work moving along.

Like the heroes in Star Wars, working alongside others can improve your odds of success. Having a friend or spouse to help will make the work easier and usually more fun. If you can get someone to help with your project it will help with motivation, as they will often provide feedback and positive reinforcement. Knowing someone is going to be there to help also makes it harder to make excuses for not showing up to work on the project. Having the right helper can be a great motivator and help make the work more fun.

▲ The reward at the end of the rainbow.

Maintaining the big picture can help keep up the inspiration as well. I sometimes like to cruise the Net in down times to look at blogs where others are working on or have finished their project boats. Sometimes just looking at other boats like mine to see how those owners have fitted out their boats can be inspiring. The Internet can be helpful in being able to visualize your finished project which in turn will keep the motivation strong. Blogging or sharing your project in online forums and groups can also be a good way to stay motivated. You will get lots of positive feedback and suggestions through this type of community. There will also be some negative feedback but it has been my experience that those are few and best just left ignored. Posting your progress and building a small following online will also keep you motivated to get work done so you can, of course, show it off.

There is a catch to the Internet, though, in that at times it will use up time better spent working on the boat. Distractions are not your friend when it comes to working on a boat restoration. It can be hard to fight these off at times. Friends and family will want your time and there will be times when the Internet seems like more fun. Some distractions can be good and it helps to take breaks to unwind. You do have to be careful of getting too easily distracted, though. For me one of the worst distractions has always been the curious dock strollers or other boat owners wandering by to see what I am up to. Although they mean well, they can easily take a lot of time out of a busy schedule. I try not to be rude and confess I enjoy chatting with folks but try to make a rule not to give them too much time. I try to set a limit of about five to ten minutes for chatting before politely excusing myself to get back to work. The regulars soon figure this out and know that our conversations will be short but they do not seem to mind. In the end I think they respect that I am trying to get things done. Distractions can come in many forms other than the guy in the boat next to you. Just keep in mind they are there and try not to get pulled off course too often.

A good way to avoid distractions or maybe work around them is to plan out each day before starting. I like to make a short list of just what I want to get done that day. I try to keep this realistic. Maybe make the list just a little longer than I think I can get done just in case I get more done than I thought I would which does happen sometimes. By keeping the list longer, if I get hung up on something I have something else to work on until I can get back on track. Making this list before starting also helps get my mind set for the day's activities, helping me keep focused as well as prepared. This also helps to plan what tools and parts I will likely need for the day as I mentally go over what I will be doing.

Interestingly enough, I saved the subject of procrastination as the last thing to talk about in this chapter. As I am sure we all know procrastination is one of the biggest hurtles to get over. We all procrastinate, some more than others, it is all too easy to do. There are these little voices in our heads that like to tell us that we can just do this or that later, when the weather is better, or when we have

▲ It will never get done like this.

more time, or the stars are better aligned, you get the point. I like to think of these little voices as monkeys in my head trying to get me to do anything but what I should be doing. There is really only one thing to do about this and that is to tell the monkeys to just shut up and let you get on with things. Of course this is easier said than done. I find most procrastination is in the form of distractions. You know you tell yourself you are just going to check your email real quick, and three hours later you realize you have been watching YouTube videos rather than getting that fiberglass work done.

So how do you avoid procrastination? First, you have to recognize when you are doing it. If you find you are making excuses for not doing something for any reason this is a sure sign of procrastinating. Instead of giving in, think about those excuses and work around them. Most of the time they are pretty lame anyway, like "I'm not really in the mood to paint today" or "There is a neat new TV show on and I really want to see it." This is why it is important to set goals, make lists, remain focused and self-disciplined. You need to be able to tell those monkeys to just leave you alone so you can get on with your work. This might also be a good time to use the reward system and tell the monkeys that if you get your list done you can watch the show you missed on DVR or perhaps later enjoy a little extra time with friends.

Staying motivated is not always easy but it is a key to getting through any boat restoration. It takes a bit of work in itself; the larger the project the more important it is. Take time to remind yourself of the end goal and the big picture. When needed, take a break to regroup and refresh. Reward yourself for getting things done but be prepared for things going wrong. Do not fall into the trap of doing less and less work until you find you are no longer working on the boat. Leave time for family and friends as these are important. Keep the work fun when possible; see if family or friends can help at times to make the work more fun. Find whatever tricks it takes to keep

▲ It's a long road but worth it.

moving forward, and in the end you will have the satisfaction of having completed something most wish they could do. You will have restored a boat you can be proud of and one that will hopefully give you many hours of pleasure.

Project Boat Resources

General information on older boats

FiberGlassics is a good online resource for smaller classic fiberglass boat information.
   http://www.fiberglassics.com/

Where to purchase project boats

Boat Angel is a group that accepts donations and resells older boats. They usually list boats on eBay.
   http://www.boatangel.org/

Cooper Capital Specialty Salvage is a larger craft salvage disposal and insurance reseller.
   http://www.cooperss.com/

USAuctions.com is an insurance reseller of all sizes and types. They usually sell on eBay but have upcoming listings online.
   http://www.usauctions.com/

YachtSalvage.com is another insurance reseller of all sizes and types.
   http://www.yachtsalvage.com/

EBay has several categories of used boats for sale. Many insurance and liquidation companies will sell through eBay as well as many individual sellers looking to sell their boats quickly.
   http://www.ebay.com/

Identification information

For US Coast Guard (USCG) documentation information, you can enter a document number or boat name to get the owner's information, but only if the boat is, or has been documented.
   http://www.st.nmfs.noaa.gov/st1/CoastGuard/VesselByID.html

The USCG also has a site that allows you to find out the manufacturer of a boat by the Hull Identification Number (HIN). This will allow you to find who built a boat based of the first three digits of the HIN.

http://uscgboating.org/content/manufacturers-identification.php

The HIN should be located on the upper starboard transom corner but is sometimes near the hull or deck. You may have to look around a bit.

http://www.boatsafe.com/nauticalknowhow/hin.html

Online forums

There are many online forums or social groups specializing in boat repair as well as owners groups for different brands of boats. These can be a great resource for anyone working on an older production boat. Facebook is also a good place to look for owners and general boat repair groups. There are far too many of these online groups to list here. Try doing a search for your boat or one you are interested in and I'm sure you will find lots of useful information.

Valuations

Estimating the value of a boat is not easy. The larger the boat the harder it gets. For small runabouts and the like, sites like NADA and Blue Book are helpful but may require a subscription.

http://www.nadaguides.com/Boats
http://www.abos.com/

I have found using Yacht World's online listing search to be a good way to see what similar boats are selling for. Although this will only give you listed prices you can take generally 10 to 20 percent off to estimate actual sales prices. Of course this will vary with the type of boat and market conditions.

http://www.yachtworld.com/

For classic boats and specialty boats you may have to do a bit more research. Check online owners groups and companies that specialize in that type of boat.

Planning and budgeting

The software is needed first. Many computers have Microsoft Office installed and this is one of the most popular office suites. If you do not have MS Office there is a free copy called OpenOffice which is available for both Windows and Mac OS computers. There is also a portable version for iPhone and Andriods.

 https://www.openoffice.org/

There are several sites that have free spreadsheet and budgeting templates for planning and controlling. As these sites tend to come and go I will not list any but a few quick searches and I am sure you can find what you need. Try a couple to find what works best for you.

Used boat parts

EBay and Amazon are popular sources. Here are some others:
 http://sailorman.com/
 http://donsmarinesalvageyard.com/
 http://www.usedsailboatparts.com/
 http://www.usedboatequipment.com/

Keep in mind websites come and go and some change URLs so not all of the above may work by the time you read this. There will likely be some new resources to check. This list will be updated from time to time on my site:
 http://www.projectboatzen.com/